Smart Mama, Smart Money

DISCARD

Also by Rosalyn Hoffman

Bitches on a Budget

Smart MAMA, Smart MONEY

Raising Happy, Healthy Kids Without Breaking the Bank

Rosalyn Hoffman

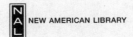
NEW AMERICAN LIBRARY

NEW AMERICAN LIBRARY
Published by New American Library, a division of
Penguin Group (USA) Inc., 375 Hudson Street,
New York, New York 10014, USA
Penguin Group (Canada), 90 Eglinton Avenue East, Suite 700, Toronto,
Ontario M4P 2Y3, Canada (a division of Pearson Penguin Canada Inc.)
Penguin Books Ltd., 80 Strand, London WC2R 0RL, England
Penguin Ireland, 25 St. Stephen's Green, Dublin 2,
Ireland (a division of Penguin Books Ltd.)
Penguin Group (Australia), 250 Camberwell Road, Camberwell, Victoria 3124,
Australia (a division of Pearson Australia Group Pty. Ltd.)
Penguin Books India Pvt. Ltd., 11 Community Centre, Panchsheel Park,
New Delhi - 110 017, India
Penguin Group (NZ), 67 Apollo Drive, Rosedale, Auckland 0632,
New Zealand (a division of Pearson New Zealand Ltd.)
Penguin Books (South Africa) (Pty.) Ltd., 24 Sturdee Avenue,
Rosebank, Johannesburg 2196, South Africa

Penguin Books Ltd., Registered Offices:
80 Strand, London WC2R 0RL, England

First published by New American Library,
a division of Penguin Group (USA) Inc.

First Printing, March 2012
10 9 8 7 6 5 4 3 2 1

 REGISTERED TRADEMARK—MARCA REGISTRADA

LIBRARY OF CONGRESS CATALOGING-IN-PUBLICATION DATA:
Hoffman, Rosalyn.
Smart mama, smart money: raising happy, healthy kids without breaking the bank/
Rosalyn Hoffman.
p. cm.
ISBN 978-0-451-23559-6
1. Child rearing.   2. Children's paraphernalia—Costs.   3. Children's clothing—Costs.
4. Home economics—Accounting.   5. Consumer education.   I. Title.
HQ769.H7182   2012
649'.1—dc23   2011044649

Set in Cochin
Designed by Catherine Leonardo

Printed in the United States of America

PUBLISHER'S NOTE
While the author has made every effort to provide accurate telephone numbers and
Internet addresses at the time of publication, neither the publisher nor the author assumes
any responsibility for errors, or for changes that occur after publication. Further, publisher
does not have any control over and does not assume any responsibility for author or third-
party Web sites or their content.

ALWAYS LEARNING   PEARSON

For Allie and Julia

ACKNOWLEDGMENTS

As I wrote *Smart Mama, Smart Money* and disappeared for weeks on end to review and relive (often painfully) my own parenting successes and failures, I came to appreciate more fully the intergenerational dialogue that informs who we are as moms. So I thank my two beautiful and brainy daughters, Allie and Julia, and my dear mom, Ruth, may she rest in peace, for all they taught me. Thanks also to my husband, Warren, for his endless encouragement, for keeping the fridge stocked, and for putting the meals on the table! I am grateful to Brooke Rogers, Cara Nelson, Rachel Dratch, and Marnie Gale, who generously offered up their fresh advice on all things baby. My thanks to the same team who so ably guided me through my first book, *Bitches on a Budget*, for their clear thinking and patient guidance as *Smart Mama, Smart Money* incubated: my editor at NAL, Tracy Bernstein; my teacher and friend Sarah Braunstein; and my agent, Alanna Ramirez.

CONTENTS

PART 3

TEACHING THE PLEASURE OF FOOD:
A New Way, a New Day

PART 4

SMART MAMAS ARE SMART ABOUT MONEY:
Get Control of Your Finances (and Pass It On)

PART 5

TECHNOMOMS:
Take a Zettabyte Out of Life

FOREWORD

WELCOME, MAMA!

Ah, the parenthood industrial complex. It preys on your fears. It permeates your dreams. It picks your pocket. You must purchase this deluxe baby-brain-exercising doodad or your child is sure to bomb the SATs! You must have a custom-designed, celebrity-endorsed organic diaper bag or your outing with baby is sure to be calamitous! You must sign them up for an ever-escalating array of classes and clinics, equip them with all the cutting-edge gadgets and gizmos, dress them in the latest fashions and fads— or they're doomed to fail.

You need *this*. You must enroll in *that*. You can't do *that*! You must read *this* and *this* and *this*. (Oh, you haven't read *that*? And you call yourself a good, responsible parent?) You must forgo yourself for your child. If you love your child, you must spend, spend, spend, spend. Right?

Wait, not so fast . . . Take a deep breath. Relax.

BE A SMART-MONEY MAMA

In the bestselling *Bitches on a Budget*—the handbook for chic living—we showed you how to edit the good from the bad, where to shop, when to buy, and how to enjoy the free pleasures life has to offer. The end result? Smarter shopping decisions. Bigger savings. Better living. We were your shopping adviser, grooming consultant, travel agent, decorator, and therapist all rolled into one! Now we're back with a book *just for moms*. From cradle to college we've shopped the world, made the meals, balanced the books, mastered the technology, and charted the courses to give you the goods on finding what your kids need without losing your shirt . . . or your sanity!

Whether you're expecting your first baby (congratulations!) or have a house full of kids, *Smart Mama, Smart Money* is the guide for parents minding their wallets *and* their values. We'll show you how a modern mom streamlines and simplifies. She doesn't waste time or money chasing after perfect lessons, fancy toys, and pricey duds. She weeds out the silly and excessive (your baby does not need a touch-screen tablet, and your teen does not need to go to Bora Bora to do community service!) from the must-haves and the must-dos. *Smart Mama, Smart Money* has the advice you need to find the right toys, gadgets, clothes, food, and lessons—all at affordable prices.

SMART DRESSING

Dressing kids takes a big bite out of every family budget. Not only do the little rug rats keep growing, but styles keep changing and their tastes keep shifting. We'll give you the rundown on all things fashion: from which stores and online sites to shop, to when hand-me-downs rock, to why you need to let your kids dress to express themselves. (Yes, we know it's tough. But you can't be a total control freak about everything.) Whatever the size of your bank account, today's hippest mom goes both ways: She is both a buyer and a seller of new and used clothing and gear. It's budget-friendly, green, and easier than you think!

SMART MONEY

In this new economy, it's critical to live within your means. *Smart Mama, Smart Money* will help you take stock of your finances, get your budget in order, and give you a primer for teaching your little ones money smarts. (You do want them to be able to afford to move out of the house one day, right?) You need to be savvy about balancing the books, credit and credit cards, interest and interest rates. Don't waste your time trying to decipher the secret handshake for college entry: There is none. Instead, you should be thinking ahead and *saving* for college—and retirement.

We'll give you an accounting.

SMART EATING

It's a mom's job to teach her children healthy eating habits, and to instill in them a reverence for the food they eat and the people who grow it. With childhood obesity nearing epidemic proportions, it's time to get the processed junk out of your grocery cart. It's also time to quit fast-food meals on the fly. Eating well is good for them and *easy on your wallet*. We'll give you the skinny on where to shop and what to buy. Don't worry; we know you're busy—we've got strategies for putting great, healthy food on the table.

SMART WIRED

Ning, Bing, Ping, Google+, Facebook, Foursquare, tweets and Twitter—it's hard enough to keep up in real space, let alone cyberspace. *Smart Mama, Smart Money* gives you the updates you need to harness the power of technology and social media, so you can keep connected and stay one step ahead of your techno-wizards. We've got the scoop on how to save money on all things wired and how to keep your kids safe in the virtual world.

SMART FUN

Is your anxiety meter through the roof as you watch other moms schlepping kids to lessons and classes? Does your kid have no one to play with because her friends are at gymnastics on Monday, violin on Tuesday, ballet on Wednesday, math tutor on Thursday, soccer all weekend? What do the other parents know that you don't? Relax. Kids need balanced schedules: time to be bored and find their own inner resources, time to ride their bikes and shoot hoops, time to experience the joy of free play. When it's time to sign them up for organized activities we offer *sane* guidance for navigating the world of lessons and programs; we'll show you how to get them set up in everything from art to music to sports to camp.

SMART VALUES

Kids need loads of things. Things they outgrow—fast. Kids want lots of things. Things they get tired of—fast. Teaching them to separate their *needs* from their *wants* and to decode the messages the media uses to sell them junk—junk they probably don't need—is part of your job. This will save you money and teach them how to be savvy consumers. In today's world, keeping in mind *what* you value is as critical as finding values—we won't let you lose focus.

It's not easy being a parent. In fact, we think it is the hardest job in the world. There is no manual, no outline, no one right way to do things (except our way, of course). Modern moms and modern families come in all shapes and sizes: single moms, married moms, divorced moms, divorced and remarried moms, stepmoms, adoptive moms, mom and moms (and dad and dads), working moms, stay-at-home moms. You're all welcome here.

Tuck the little ones in, sit down with a glass of wine (you deserve it), and start reading about how to raise happy, healthy kids who can navigate the real world of junk food and junk television. Kids who know how to read a Web site for the hustle; how to sew on a button; how to grow a tomato; how to sauce the pasta. Kids who know how to play and have fun.

Sign The Smart Mama
MANIFESTO*

- We will call what we're doing *work.* Even if the world doesn't acknowledge it, we will: Motherhood is the hardest work in the world. It's physically demanding, psychologically strenuous, spiritually complex, and unpaying.

- We will cry when we need to.

- We will laugh maniacally when we need to.

- We will complain when we need to. We are allowed to bitch. We'll never forget the healing power of a good old-fashioned rant.

- We will boast unapologetically. Yes, our child *is* the cutest, smartest, most hilarious, most cuddly on the block.

- While our kids *are* the cutest, smartest, most delightful creatures ever planted on this earth, we will not turn them into our status symbols of success.

- We will not forget to play. With our kids and by ourselves.

- We will not spend money haphazardly, or on useless status objects, or on stuff we think we "should" have.

- We will ask for help when we need it.

- We will share with other moms by taking delight in their children and by offering a helping hand when they need it.

- We will yell when we need to and feel guilty later.

- We will do our best to educate ourselves, to read valuable books, to attend parenting classes and lectures, to listen to those "experts" we admire—but we will also *trust our instincts.*

- We will avoid the polarizing black-and-white thinking that pervades the media. We know people raise children in different ways.

- We will forgive ourselves when we make mistakes.

- We will share our triumphs, fears, and hopes with other parents.

- We will teach our children to accept everyone for who they are and to rejoice in the differences in the people around them.

- We will not forget the important role that fathers play, or deny fathers their own wisdom or their own experience (despite our threats to call child welfare because of their incessant need to toss the kid over their heads).

- We will be strong, smart role models—in our successes and in our failures.

- We will find places of sanity and sanctuary in our own backyard, the library, the nature preserve, and, on occasion, the mall.

- We will not forget who we are.

- We will be honest with ourselves about who our children are.

- We will let our children see us as human beings.

- We will remember that we are *not* our children. We will let them live their own lives without too much meddling.

- We will learn from our children. Their innocence, naïveté, and carefree outlook are inspiring.

- We will remember to find joy in each day no matter what the challenges are ahead of us. (And just in case we can't find the joy—no matter how hard we try—we will keep a bottle of sauvignon blanc chilled and ready in the fridge.)

*We've made this list with help from our fans. Join us at *SmartMama SmartMoney.com* to add your rules to the Smart Mama Manifesto!

PART 1

IN THE BEGINNING:
A Preview . . .

INTRODUCTION

If you're a mama in waiting or a newly minted mama (congrats!), we're here to give you a preview. If you've already survived the early years feel free to skip ahead, or stay with us for a few pages as we begin to offer the support and guidance you need to navigate the Kiddie Perfecting Complex. Let's face facts. You are (or will soon be) assaulted by a constant shrill barrage of messages: Buy this/think this/do this (*not that!*) or you're doomed to be a terrible, horrible, no-good, very bad parent.

Hold on, mamas. Look around. Contrary to popular opinion, the sky is not falling.

Start with this basic premise: You don't need most of the sh*t these hustlers are pushing. You do not need a special wipe warmer, a special nose-blower, or handmade Italian baby furniture. Mommy and Me classes are great for connecting with other new moms, but don't kid yourself—your newborn couldn't care less. Don't spend money believing he will get a head start in tiny-tot gym or percussion class. (A head start on what, by the way?)

Classical music delivered in utero and Baby Einstein DVDs will not make her a smart, healthy, happy human being.

In fact, you can't "make" a human being—well, technically you did—but you can't "make" your child into the person you think he should be (or the person you want him to be) by buying him stuff. There is no buying happiness, and there is no buying being a good mama.

1

BABIES ARE NOT ALIENS

For aeons kids have grown up to lead happy and successful adult lives without benefit of newborn video monitors, Kumon math, and the must-haves as defined by "the Gwyneth" and her GOOP. A diaper bag by any other name is a messenger bag, a shoulder bag, a big canvas bag. A changing table is any safe, flat surface you can lay a squirmy little bundle on. Don't get brainwashed into believing that all things related to having a baby in the house need to be made especially for a baby. This is a modern market and merchandising phenomenon with one goal: to sell you products that will ultimately bust your budget.

Don't get us wrong; we're not killjoys. Every new mom should take pleasure in the adorableness of babydom. Setting up a nursery is exciting. Dressing them in showstopper outfits is fun. Remember, though, they grow fast, and before you know it they won't need a "special" diaper changing surface, and that killer outfit won't fit.

STAY ON BUDGET

You need to be wise about who gets into your wallet, because there's a lot more expense ahead of you—estimates are that during her first seventeen years your cute bundle of joy will cost around $230K. This won't be easy. The entire *kinder*-product industry is trying to bust your budget by preying on your God-given insecurities and worries. They'll offer every hustle known to man, from sandals for newborns (have you ever seen an infant walking?) to shopping cart covers (did your mom put a cover on the supermarket cart when you rode in it?) to tutoring for three-year-olds (so ridiculous, even we're speechless).

While you most assuredly need an occasional splurge on killer heels and martinis, your tot definitely does *not* need Little Marc Jacobs shoes at two hundred bucks a pop, plastic dinosaurs spitting out forgettable factoids, or toys marketed to "gifted" babies. Every baby is gifted. The only thing not "gifted" is the parent who buys this crap.

A modern mom streamlines and simplifies. This is good for the earth and good for your budget. Remember the old adage that less is more? Make this your mantra as you begin your journey into provisioning and raising baby.

BEING A GOOD MAMA IS NOT FOR SALE: THE SOFT STUFF

It can be lonely being a new mom. You're often alone with a baby whose rhythms and needs are inscrutable. You're sleep deprived and in hormonal flux, which makes each cry, shriek, and gurgle pierce you to the quick. You're obsessed by poop and sleep. Your old friends can't relate. Life has changed: no more carefree flea market excursions, late-night rendezvous for wine, spontaneous vacations, double features. In fact, you'd give anything just to take a shower in peace. You're assuming a new identity, one laden with new responsibility, but chances are you've yet to establish a new support network. Exhausted, confused, and consumed by all things baby, you may find the lure of the stores and the call to tiny-tot classes promise both a way out of the house and sorely needed companionship.

All of this is dangerous to your bank account. Yes, you need company. We are not encouraging you to be hermits! The goal? To find *free pleasures* that connect you with the outside world.

That said, there's a truth that can't be denied: When your kid is screaming or in pain (or you're screaming and in pain), you'll do anything . . .buy anything . . .go anywhere to make it stop. We've spent $75 on a fancy lightweight cotton blanket to safely swaddle baby during a heat wave. Seventy-five dollars? Insane, right? And yet this particular bundle of joy wouldn't sleep unless she was . . . well, *bundled*. When temps climbed toward the triple digits and the heat-rashy kid wouldn't doze until tightly swaddled . . . out came the credit card. (Do we regret this? For God's sake, no. Well, maybe just a little . . .)

The point? In your quest to cure colic or get a good night's sleep, you'll be sucked into the baby superstores. You'll be tempted to purchase fifty different night-lights, lullaby CDs, pacifiers, and swings and slings. Try, as much as possible, to wait it out. To borrow stuff. To keep your head. To take deep breaths. If you do buy, keep your receipts (half those slings and swings will make the colic worse).

You'll also be tempted to join the band of moms seeking to raise child prodigies through, say, early music classes. While singing and playing together is joyful, do you really need someone teaching you how to play and sing with your baby? (For a reminder of how "Itsy Bitsy Spider" goes, visit YouTube.)

This is just the beginning. It's your introduction to the world of thinking you can buy solutions to all your parenting problems, that you can buy your way into being a good mama, that you can buy your way out of teething trouble, that you can buy a community, that you can buy genius.

THE BLOGOSPHERE: Mommy Beware

AS YOU'RE TRYING to sift and sort which products to buy, what lessons to do, whom to trust, be wary of blogs featuring ads for the same products they're reviewing. We've seen too many "best" baby product lists that aren't well researched or thought out but have simply been posted in order to get advertising on the site.

A WARM-UP LESSON (SEE MORE IN PART VI)

You do not need for-pay classes for your six-month-old. But you do have to stay busy. You do have to start making connections with other moms. Start by asking at the hospital about new-mother groups in the area. Call your local church, mosque, or synagogue and see what they offer for new moms and tots. Ditto the local community center. Scour the local parenting paper. Ask people you meet at the playground. Whether it's joining a group run by a local agency or finding a few compatible new parents and starting your own group, you need to make new friends with whom to share the joys and worries. This will be your salvation.

CONNECT FOR FREE

MEETUP.COM IS A friend-making, sanity-saving Web site if there ever was one. It's a fantastic resource for moms looking to build community. Specify your town. Specify your interest. Rather than join, you can create your own group. Are you a mom over thirty-five looking for others in your age group? Do you want to find other hiking, biking, cooking, or bird-watching moms? Are you a mom of a kid with special needs? Twins? Triplets? Send out a call.

When our kids were tots, we were desperate for adult stimulation, so we organized a book group of moms with infants. While the babies nursed, cried, and slept, we'd talk about the book—though of course this part never lasted too long. Each meeting inevitably turned to our worries about our own bodies and their awkward changes—episiotomies, weight gain, weight loss, sex, no sex—and then, of course, to our obsession with our infants. Who had a good pediatrician and who didn't; when did they recommend solids and what did they recommend? We shared worries about the kid who wouldn't roll over, the kid who was off the growth chart, the kid who had a reverse sleep clock. This core group of moms stuck together and, as the kids grew, it became a "real" playgroup of five moms and their tykes. Sometimes we would convene as a group at the local playground or town swimming pool; other times we would trade off minding the kids. Several moms at a time would watch the five kids. This was a lifesaver.

BOOKS FOR NEW MOMS

In My Mother's House by Kim Chernin

Battle Hymn of the Tiger Mother by Amy Chua

Momma Zen by Karen Maezen Miller

Mothers Who Think: Tales of Real-life Parenthood by Camille Peri, Kate Moses

The Mommy Myth by Susan Douglas and Meredith Michaels

Operating Instructions by Anne Lamott

The Sweet Relief of Missing Children by Sarah Braunstein (If you want to connect with the darker part of the whole child-raising endeavor, or you fear you're losing your edge.)

REAL AND SIMPLE: THE HARD STUFF

While every mom wants to do the best she can for her baby, remember that an *Elle Decor*–worthy nursery means nothing to a child. The toy-gadget-gizmo parade will not amp up her learning ability or musical talent or athletic prowess. Nor will an excessive amount of junk distract and entertain her in proportion to the amount of time you will spend keeping it organized. While we urge you to go to resale, to be an eager recipient of hand-me-downs, and to buy on sale, our best advice is to just say no to most things. It's smart to start spare and add in only as need demands. And while we advise splurging on investment-grade pieces for adults, the opposite holds true for kiddies. Invest only in high-use and safety-related items. Everything else is disposable.

THE CAMERA

TECHNICALLY NOT A baby item, this is one investment-worthy piece of equipment. The pricey pram, sheets, and nursery curtains will be in the dustbin before you know it. But while you believe you'll remember every precious moment, you won't. The years zero through three are a big blur. Get a great camera and document them. (Just be careful not to turn into one of "those" people always behind the camera videoing everything and missing the real moment.)

We've just invested in the Canon PowerShot S95—awesome.

2

THE NURSERY AND OTHER GEAR

When outfitting a nursery, think hard about what a baby really needs. They are babies for a blink of an eye, and unless you're planning on a modern-day *Cheaper by the Dozen,* the shelf life of nursery furnishings is short. Outside of the crib, buy all the other furniture for baby's room with your soon-to-be toddler, grade schooler, middle schooler, even high schooler in mind. Do not go to overpriced baby or juvenile furniture stores to shop. A bureau is a chest of drawers is a bureau, whether it's sold at a baby store or a regular furniture store.

We're also not in favor of pricey convertible cribs. Keep it simple. When the time comes for them to move to a real big-boy or big-girl bed, get them just that—a real bed. Think about it: When they enter their generation's version of the Goth or heavy metal phase, will they really want their headboard from the convertible crib? Yes, ladies, your babies will soon have "images" to protect.

All you need to make the nursery cozy, adorable, and original is a little sweat equity and an assortment of well-chosen accessories. Paint the walls a great color. Splurge on things like fun lampshades or hip wall appliqués or crafty hangings. Find one-of-a-kind handmade art and decorations on Etsy. Register for (meaning: get your friends to buy) out-of-your-budget nursery centerpieces like an expensive mobile.

RECORD YOUR GREED

THE BABY REGISTRY is a onetime gift-with-baby that you should shamelessly publicize to all your friends and family. Be smart about what you register for, and feel free to refer them to our Web site (smartmamasmartmoney.com) for the article on how smart it is for family and friends to chip in to buy really *big* gifts. (Things like that ridiculous stroller you know you shouldn't buy but secretly covet.)

While each store will tempt you with wonder, pick one or two and consolidate your wish lists with them. Just be certain to select hassle-free stores that make it easy to return and exchange gifts.

Make curtains from whimsical fabrics. Buy unpainted furniture pieces, then paint and jazz them up yourself: Stencil on purple butterflies, red trucks, yellow stars, cows jumping over the moon. Repaint as they grow. Shop at flea markets and yard sales. Look for old dressers, bookcases, armoires and restore them. In our house, an ornate nineteenth-century bureau (from a used furniture store) held everything from diapers to onesies to receiving blankets. It lasted from infancy until college—and it cost $75. Find, buy, fix—then when your kiddo leaves the nest, resell the pieces yourself.

While on the furniture hunt, keep your eyes peeled for a

toddler-sized table and chairs for the nursery (if there's room) or another spot in the house, so once they're big enough to color and draw and do projects they have their own pint-size place.

Not handy, crafty, or flea friendly?

Head over to IKEA and buy very good-looking (though hard to assemble, not exactly ecofriendly, and disposable), *dirt-cheap* furniture.

EMBED RECALLS

IT SEEMS THERE is an almost daily deluge of consumer product recalls for baby gear. It's up to you to stay up-to-date on these. It's also up to you to exercise common sense when buying products for your family. Just because a product is on the shelf at the store doesn't mean it's guaranteed to be safe. If it's a crib, look at the way it's put together; give it a shake, a rattle, a roll. If it's not sturdy, or has obvious rough spots or loose fittings, don't buy it. Keep in mind that your baby will be putting everything in his mouth. Look at every toy, book, and article of clothing in terms of its suitability to gnaw on. There should be no lead in the paint, no phthalates in the plastic. No small parts that might detach and pose a choking hazard, including those socks and tees with cute little doodads and doohickeys; we can't tell you how many recalls we've seen for items of this sort. Be smart. Be responsible. Trust your own instincts. Buy from reputable makers. Keep up-to-date on product recalls, and before you buy any used product, check in first with:

The Consumer Product Safety Commission: http://www
.cpsc.gov/index.html

The Consumer Product Safety Commission mobile app for Android: http://apps.usa.gov/product-recalls-2/

THE GEAR

When it comes to most tiny-tot gear, we're in favor of hand-me-down and flea market finds, but there are certain items you should *not* buy secondhand. Topping the list are car seats, cribs, and baby bedding.

KEEP UP-TO-DATE

CRIB AND CAR seat models change frequently, so do your homework to find the safest and the best value. It's pretty simple: Plug into up-to-the-minute chatter on mom networks like iVillage, BabyCenter, Babble, and Mamapedia. Check out *Consumer Reports* and the latest edition of *Baby Bargains*.

THE CRIB

You must buy a new crib. In June 2011 the Consumer Product Safety Commission issued stringent new safety standards. These new regulations require sturdier construction, stronger hardware, and more rigorous product testing for all cribs. Drop-sided cribs may no longer be sold. When you go out shopping make certain that you choose a crib with the following labels: 16 CFR 1219 (full-size cribs) and 16 CFR 1220 (non-full-size cribs).

Buy the least expensive well-put-together crib out there (think IKEA), but splurge on an organic mattress. Yes, you need to buy a new mattress, one that snugly fits inside the crib. Baby will spend more time in the crib than anywhere else, and the less he is exposed to off-gassing and fumes from mattress components like formaldehyde, phthalates, polyurethane foam, PBDEs and other chemicals, the better.

As for bedding, buy 100 percent cotton sheets with a high

thread count, full elastic bottom, and no nylon in any of the stitching. These will be washed and rewashed, so you want them to hold up over time, with no dangerous shrinkage or unraveling in any place. Buy Buy Baby (Bed Bath & Beyond for minis) and the Land of Nod (Crate & Barrel for minis) have cute sheets at all price points. Think of it this way: Since baby bumpers and quilts are now verboten as smothering hazards, sheets may be the place to liven up baby's room with a spot of sweet or zesty color.

The other item that goes in the crib at sleep time is the swaddle blanket. Aden & Anais muslin swaddle blankets get high grades. We found great prices for them at both Bed Bath & Beyond and on the "flash sale mob" (see page 71). While we're on the topic of linens, a word about towels. Remember we said babies are not aliens? Well, we don't get the special hooded baby towel. How long do they wear it, anyway? A baby is simply a little person. A little person who is briefly wet. A towel is a towel. No need to buy precious pricey ones for little precious.

ROCK ON, MAMA

FIND A COMFY rocker—old or new—and buy it. This will take you far—from the sleepless nights of hourly nursing, to soothing earaches and nightmares with a hundred renditions of "Rock-a-bye Baby," to cozy nights reading *Goodnight Moon*, *The Lady with the Alligator Purse*, or *Animal Cafe*. We love the look of old rockers . . . those pastel-hued upholstered gliders we can do without. Our rule of thumb? If it's not a piece of furniture you'd want in your house after baby grows up, skip it. But that's just us. Get whatever works for you, and then rock to your heart's content.

THE CAR SEAT

A car seat is one of the few things that really can be called a matter of life and death. Do not buy used car seats; they may not meet modern safety standards, and the wear and tear they've endured can impair their functioning. Say thanks, but no, thanks, to hand-me-downs. The incidence of kids getting killed in car crashes is staggering. Don't screw around here. No savings are worth it. Period.

Before you begin shopping for car seats, go online to the National Highway Transportation Safety Administration's Web site (nhtsa.gov). Read their latest recommendations and advisories for car seats and locate the nearest agency that will do a car seat safety check in your area. Three out of four seats are not correctly installed, so before baby comes home, head over to have them show you how to secure your new seat properly. The NHTSA's most recent advisory is that you start with a rear-facing seat for your infant, move to a front-facing seat for your toddler, and move to a booster seat for your grade-school kid. (Don't be confused by front- and back-facing—all kids should ride in the rear seat of your vehicle.)

Do your homework, since models keep changing. (As of this writing the Chicco KeyFit gets high marks for safety and price.) Once you identify the right one for you, go online to compare multiple retailers' pricing; if you find a good deal online, make sure you factor in taxes and shipping cost.

Remember to go online and register baby's new car seat, so that the manufacturer can directly inform you of recalls. Other than safety-related items, everything else you might need is up for begging, borrowing, or stealing—uh, not really. We are a little prissy about used diapers, underwear, and breast pumps, but that's just us. We have friends who insist that all the "intimate" parts on the pumps are disposable, and cloth diapers can be sterilized.

THE STROLLER(S)

Oh, my God. Strollers. It's more complicated buying a first stroller than it is buying a new car. So we'll make it simple.

Will you be in and out of the car? Don't buy heavy or hard-to-collapse strollers. Are you a jogger? Do you walk a lot on uneven terrain—potholed streets or dirt lanes? You'll need wheels that are adapted to this. Some moms skip the whole early stroller thing and carry their tiny tots in wraps and slings instead. While we caution against too much junk and advocate keeping things simple, most suburban and urban moms end up with two strollers: a sturdy, infant-appropriate one and a lightweight umbrella one for when they're old enough to sit up.

Now think used.

Go to flea markets. Cruise suburban neighborhood yard sales. Make friends with people who are finishing up having babies. Be strategic. You know that family down the street with the third kid they're wheeling around the neighborhood? They're about to become your new best friend.

Just make sure it's sturdy. Double wheels are better than single wheels. Look at the nuts and bolts and be certain they're tight and not stripped. No rust. Make sure it's not too heavy. Folds easily. Bring your smartphone and before you waste your bucks, even if it's cheap, check for recalls. (*Always* check for recalls on secondhand stuff.)

THE FACTORY OUTLET FACTOR

FOR THOSE MAMAS in the northeast, UPPAbaby's factory outlet store rocks. Take a drive to the scenic coastal town of Hingham, Massachusetts, and score a bargain.

If only new will do, then just like a Ford Focus will get you to work on time, any decent stroller will get you to the playgroup on time. For good value, in car seat compatible models, test drive the Chicco Cortina and Graco's Vie4. Want to kick it up a notch? Look into the Mamas & Papas Sola. While its $420 price tag isn't cheap, these wheels get high marks. Just like you don't need a Bentley to get you to the grocery store, you don't need a Bugaboo or Stokke ($1,200-plus) to wheel your wee one to the park, but if you can't control yourself or you've been gifted with one, remember there is an active aftermarket. So look forward to selling it when your baby has outgrown it.

THE HIGH CHAIR

Don't spend a lot of money on a high chair. Think camp (style wise, not outdoorsy camp) when you buy one. While normally we're modern, Zen, cool kind of gals, this is allowed to be the one eye-popping centerpiece in the middle of a white, sleek, or stainless kitchen oasis. The goofier, cheesier, tackier, the better. You want vinyl; you want hellacious patterns (aka washable and stain hiding). Trust us: There is no object outside of a diaper that gets dirtier or more disgusting over time than a baby's high chair.

Want a new one? Say hello to Walmart, Target, and IKEA. (We're not big fans of Babies "R" Us. The assortments are overwhelming, the pricing not always the cheapest, the online operation and return policy not the best.)

Consider this when buying a high chair.

- When you identify a high chair you like, go online and take time to read the reviews from other moms who have purchased the same models. (Do this for any new product!)
- Keep it simple. The more features, the more money. The more features, the more likely for something to go wrong.

Get a high chair for your kiddo to sit in and throw food out of—not one that will rock her to sleep or that has four positions for reclining!

- For cheap and basic, IKEA's got you covered. Their Antilop chair is—we kid you not—twenty bucks. And you can buy an inflatable back support for when your tyke's brand-new to the world of upright dining.

High chairs are an item you can buy used. The bad/good news is that there have been a lot of high chair recalls in the past few years. The models prone to sudden collapse, dangerous pieces poking out, or strap problems have (we hope) been weeded out of the market, but exercise due diligence before you accept a secondhand one. On the other hand, keep in mind that brand-new models can get rave reviews, only to have problems emerge after they have been market-tested for a while. Stick with reputable manufacturers for your safest bet.

SECONDHAND TIP: Where Labels Count

WHEN YOU'RE BUYING used or thinking hand-me-down, make sure the original manufacturer's product identification label is somewhere on it. This will let you quickly identify whether it has been subject to safety recall.

OTHER STUFF . . . THUMBS-UP, THUMBS-DOWN

Say yes to . . .

It's impossible to know whether you're going to have the colicky baby who's only happy when he's swinging or the colicky baby who cries louder in the swing. Whether the sound machine will gently send her to sleep or enrage her. Whether he'll love the sling or it will provoke that scary, long suck-air-in-silence-will-they-ever-take-a-breath-again-red-in-the-face kind of scream.

How will you know? You won't until your son or daughter expresses their preference. This is a good thing. It's the beginning of them having their own point of view. You just need to listen.

Still, we think these are worth a try:

- Sleep Sheep white-noise machine
- Baby swing
- ERGO baby carrier
- Bouncy seat (vibration optional—it helped our finicky love)

Remember, keep your receipts and all packaging. Baby gives repeated thumbs-down? Back it goes.

Say no to . . .

Splat mats. Why spend $30 on a piece of plastic to go under the eating area? Keep a broom or a dog handy. If you have white rugs in the kitchen (you don't, we know, but just in case), go to the hardware store and get a piece of heavy-duty clear plastic cut from a long roll for a few bucks.

Special bottles of "toy and surface" cleaner for $6.99. Use your everyday nontoxic cleaners to do the job.

Baby bathtubs for $50. Use the kitchen sink.

While some of the baby paraphernalia might offer some relief, the utility is marginal, and the space it consumes and bite it takes out of your wallet is not worth it.

THE BABY MONITOR

START WITH A HAND-ME-DOWN or used baby monitor, but depending on the size of your house or the radio interference in your area, you might need to pick up a new one. Stand in the nursery and send someone to the farthest reaches of your home or yard to make sure you can pick up sounds. We can't tell you how many we cycled through before we found one that worked in our house.

Unless you have a good reason for the video monitor, we say give it a break. Do you really need eyes on baby every single second of the day? We think this device breeds the wrong kind of hypervigilance—it actually *creates* anxiety—and that baby-stuff manufacturers are exploiting new parents' fears. That said, if it makes you feel better (we know a mama of a preemie who was really reassured by her video monitor), go ahead and tune in to the baby show.

3

TOY STORY

NO OVERINDULGING!

How many homes have you walked into where kiddie junk has taken over? An entire room buried under plastic toys, stuffed animals, piles of puzzles, crates of battery-powered toys? If it's your house, be honest: It's way more stuff than any kid or parent can ever fully attend to. Right?

You don't need it all. Everything is new for a child. Whether it's playing peekaboo, pouring water from one plastic measuring cup into another, or making the same mooing sound over and over and over again, they've never seen it, heard it, or done it before. Our kids were just as happy sitting on the kitchen floor and banging on pots and pans with wooden spoons, opening and closing the cabinets, and stacking plastic containers as they were with any of the fancy-schmancy toys we had tumbling out of the playroom. Need more proof? Check out the YouTube video (http://www.youtube.com/watch?v=RP4abiHdQpc) of a dad ripping a piece of paper to send his delighted eight-month-old into endless gales of laughter.

CONTROL TOY CREEP

1. Organize a neighborhood toy swap

THE ALLURE OF a new plaything vanishes after a little while. . . . Give it a couple of weeks, a month, and the bloom is off the rose; soon that cherished Mr. Potato Head is growing extra eyes in a corner. Share him! Make some other rug rat's day—and save her mama big bucks. Later, when he's returned, your little Stephanie gets the sweet pleasure of reacquaintance.

Invite trustworthy friends to join. Label objects. Rotate in and out monthly. Sanitize. It's green, it's thrifty, and it keeps life fresh.

2. Find a community playroom

SEE IF YOUR town's high school or community center has a child development program and playroom. We have friends who have chosen not to invest in any major toy purchase, and others who don't have the room for a play kitchen or tool bench. They bring their kids to play in these centers.

Best of all, this is another free way for you and your kids to make new friends.

Sorry, Toys "R" Us—Smart "B" Us Mamas.

WHICH TOYS?

Selecting toys for your child seems a simple task—until you go out and actually look for them. The marketplace is overwhelming. The best toys are those that don't "do" the task for kids, but that kids have to figure out and use creatively. The less battery power, the more active the engagement. To collect the right mix for your kiddos, you need to understand their developmental needs at each stage of growth.

(Note: we said *collect*. Smart mamas score hand-me-down and secondhand toys.)

One way to do this is to find an independent toy store near you, stroll in with your little cutie and chat up the people who own it or work there; make them your counselors when it comes to buying toys.

A baby has simple needs: a mobile, an activity blanket, teethers, rattles, a stuffed animal, a safe baby mirror (yes, it starts young), an activity/gym bar, and small balls they can pick up, shake, and make moving parts inside "do" things. They aren't going to be riding a battery-powered VW Bug, they aren't going to be strapping on a tool belt and hammering away, and they aren't going to be pushing a baby in a tiny stroller. Wait to add these to the growing mess inside your house.

GOOD ONLINE TOY RESOURCES

WE LIKE THE following resources to help you understand which toys are developmentally appropriate and which toys are worth the money and/or space investment:

The Oppenheim Toy Portfolio (http://www.toyportfolio. com/Awards2.php)

Parent's Choice "Best 25 Toys of 25 Years" (http://www .parents-choice.org/article.cfm? art_id=347&the_ page=editorials)

Fisher-Price age-by-age Playtime Guide (http://www .fisher-price.com/fp.aspx?st=30&e=myfplanding)

A TRIM LIST

We are ashamed to admit the playroom in our house was stunningly filled with too much junk, but the following are all toys that were played with over and over again and that we would buy again:

Shape sorters and stackers

Blocks: hard and soft

LEGOs

A toy telephone

A toy computer

Dolls and a stroller

Trucks and cars

Fisher-Price "Little People"

Play-Doh

Crayons

A pull-along/push-along/sit-on truck

Wooden puzzles

Balls of all shapes and sizes

Dress-up clothes

And, space permitting:

A kitchen

A tool bench

A tiny-tot slide

A kid-powered car

SPLASH TIME: A Metaphor and a Rant

DO NOT FILL up the tub with anything but water and a few fun toys for your kid to use to play with the water. Every kid should have one rubber ducky, a set of cups to toss water around in, a floating game of ringtoss or an armada of toy boats, even a squirt gun to spray you with so they can laugh like mad. (All should be lead-free, BPA-free, phthalate-free, PVC-free.)

They do not need "educational" bath toys. Flash cards with animals that break apart and float, letters that connect to spell words and float, numbers that both adhere to the tile walls and float. Hello. Why does everyone feel the need to be "teaching" kids all the time? In the bathtub. Brushing their teeth. Going potty. Give them a break. Give yourself a break. Give us a break. Trust us, they do not need to master the alphabet and arithmetic before they walk. They do not need to do algebra before kindergarten. They do not need to do eighth-grade work in third grade. They need to *play,* and they don't need fancy toys to do this work.

While we're at it, you can't buy protection from everything in life. Spout covers for the faucet. Why? They are cute for a week and then become mildew collectors and impediments for any adult who wants to use the tub. Be cautious; teach your kids to be cautious; let her bang her head once and she won't do it again. How will she ever learn? If it's a problem, take a washcloth, wrap the faucet, and remove the cloth after bath time. Besides, it's not like you're ever leaving them all alone in the tub to smash their little noggin.

Geesh.

4

TENDER TUSHIES
AND GENTLE SOLUTIONS

A DIRTY BUSINESS

No getting around it: Babies need diapers, and lots of them. So which is best, cloth or disposable? It all depends. Cloth diapers washed at home will be your least expensive diaper choice (that is, if you don't factor in the labor cost). Plus, you'll be able to launder them in eco-friendly laundry solutions without harmful bleach—good for baby, good for Mother Earth. For many reasons, though, cloth diapers don't work for most moms, and the disposable route is a perfectly fine choice. If it fits your budget and your baby's bum, we're all for using chlorine-free and more eco-sensitive lines like Seventh Generation and Nature Babycare. As for the argument that using disposables, with their effectiveness in keeping kids dry, delays potty training—well, sounds like a load of crap to us.

In any event, cloth versus disposable is like the bottle-versus-breast or the SAHM-versus–working mom stuff—there is no right way except what works for your family. No judging allowed. Use both if it suits your lifestyle.

Which diapers? Experiment. Different bottoms, different shapes, different diapers. The best sources for savings:

- Amazon Mom: you get the benefit of Amazon Prime without the fee, 30 percent off diapers and wipes, and free two-day shipping.
- Diapers.com: good prices and assortments with free shipping on orders over $49—that's easy in the diaper business!
- Costco: we love the prices, but their assortment is limited—if they have what your kid is wearing, great. If not, shop around.

Just save yourself time and money and don't invest in lots of any single style until you're sure it's a fit for your kid's tushie. (And remember they keep growing, so don't invest in too big a quantity of any one size at once!)

USE A TRASH BAG

DIRTY DIAPERS STINK. Modern technology will not change this. Do not invest in expensive diaper pails offering olfactory relief. Go low-tech. Empty the trash.

LOTIONS AND POTIONS

Gentle baby skin cries out for salves, soaps, and lotions to cleanse, soothe, and protect it from rash, dirt, and sun. The marketplace is glutted with solutions, but with so many products available, the question is: Which to buy? The answer: the best quality you can afford. Remember everything you apply can cause a topical reaction, and everything you apply is absorbed into their system, so avoid using products loaded with irritating chemicals, potential carcinogens, and endocrine disrupters. Be particularly mindful of this when you use products that will be sitting on and seeping into their skin. Since all the lotions, potions, and cleaners can get expensive, a smart mom makes strategic buys and stocks up when products go on sale.

BUM BUMS

There is nothing sadder than a baby screaming because he has a bad diaper rash. There is no bigger indictment of your shaky new parenting skills than the sight of his precious bottom staring up at you, angry and red. If only you'd changed the diaper earlier, if you didn't wrap it so tightly, if you'd used a different brand, or cloth instead of disposables, if you'd skipped those extra-hots on your taco . . .

Don't beat yourself up, because no matter how vigilant you are about changing their diaper or how cautious you are about what products you use, at some point almost every baby gets diaper rash. As with most things, start with the simplest solution, a gentle warm-water cleaning, a soft pat dry, and a clean place for them to strut their bare bum so the fresh air can work its *free* magic.

BABY BE FREE

WHILE WE KNOW you can't police every surface, every container, every drop of product your kiddos come in contact with, try to avoid exposing them to suspect ingredients by first checking in with the EWG's Skin Deep cosmetics database before you buy new products: http://www.ewg.org/skindeep/search.php?query.

As for bottom soothers, we're big fans of both Belli Baby Protect Me Diaper Rash Cream and Burt's Bees Baby Bee Diaper Ointment, but they can get pricey. A less expensive alternative is Aquaphor Baby Healing Ointment, which we found for as little as $.97 an ounce. While zinc oxide is the key ingredient in several of the bestselling mass-market diaper ointments, you'll be surprised by how many also are made with ingredients you want to avoid—so bring your magnifying glass when you go shopping. With all baby products, patch-test a small amount to make sure your kiddo doesn't have any allergic reactions. And, of course, if a diaper rash is causing extreme pain, is oozy, or doesn't clear up in a couple of days, call your doc.

CONSULT, CONSULT, CONSULT

BEFORE YOU START applying lotions and potions, make sure you've identified the problem correctly. When in doubt always consult your pediatrician. We also like this checklist put out by the National Library of Medicine: http://www.nlm.nih.gov/medlineplus/ency/article/003259.htm.

MORE FROM THE BOTTOM UP

WIPE AND SWIPE

If you want to save the most money and be a good green queen, use a washcloth with warm water to wipe up baby's bottom. This is not a practical solution for most busy moms, though, and you'll be using your fair share of packaged baby wipes; just make sure you use products free of abrasive alcohols and artificial fragrances.

Check into Seventh Generation chlorine-free baby wipes. While some moms complain they can come out of the box a little dry, we like them because they are alcohol-, fragrance-, *and* bleach-free. We've found the refills for as little as three cents each.

TAKE A POWDER

Old-fashioned talc is a big no-no for baby. The fine particles are easily breathed in and bad for the lungs. If your doc gives using powder the thumbs-up, ask her about inexpensive arrowroot, cornstarch, or rice starch as an alternative to store-bought baby powder. Just make sure none of it goes airborne and that it doesn't turn to paste inside baby's pudgy folds.

SHAMPOO

Johnson's baby shampoo is part of an entire generation's collective memory of what a baby smells like. But nothing stays the same, so check out California Baby Shampoo & Bodywash, Peter Rabbit Organics, and Burt's Bees products for shampoo and body washes. They get high environmental and low "nasty content" test marks. While they are pricier than the old standbys, you'll be using only a microscopic amount to lather up what little hair Junior has.

CRADLE CAP

Skip pricey solutions and try gently massaging olive oil into baby's scalp. Leave it on for an hour and comb through with a fine-toothed comb. Shampoo.

SOAP

When it comes to bath time, use warm water and the same simple shampoo/body wash you're using on baby's hair. Remember you're not bathing infants daily (too drying), not letting them sit in bubbly water (too irritating), and they're so tiny you're not using up much product. Once our kids were a year old we started washing them up with the same bar soap the whole family used (Dove unscented).

As far as laundry stuff goes, we used unscented everyday laundry detergent until we had one baby with really sensitive skin. Then we switched to special detergent just for her wash. Skip fabric softener and dryer sheets (for your tots and your family)—we think they are a waste of money.

BLOW OFF THE BUBBLES

No bubble baths. Period. Save money. Delight your kiddo by blowing bubbles if you must, but save them skin and genital irritation.

ANTI-ANTIBACTERIAL SOAP

FIRST OF ALL, you don't need a zero-tolerance bacterial environment. There are some good bacteria that everyone needs. Second, killing off too much bacteria is leading to antibiotic-resistant strains—don't leave that legacy for your kids. Finally, many of the antibacterial soaps and lotions are made from really, really nasty ingredients.

A BABY IN THE SUN

Tiny babies should be kept out of the sun, but as they get older you'll need to be thoughtful, and a bit of a nag about what they wear, the kind of sunscreen used, and its frequency of application. Stand firm on keeping your kiddos out of harm's way during the midday blaze, when the sun is at its zenith and most dangerous. If you are out picnicking, camping, or at the beach, make it naptime and invest in a good-quality beach umbrella or tent.

Buying sunscreen is tricky. There are so many on the market, and the ingredients vary from product to product. What you must buy are blocks that are PABA-free with SPF 30 broad-spectrum protection (UVA and UVB protection). There is no such thing as a waterproof sunscreen, and we're still trying to figure out exactly what water resistant means—so if your kiddo is in and out of the wading pool, be vigilant in reapplying the block. Be vigilant even if she's not in and out of the wading pool. While it's easier to apply, skip the spray-on stuff; the fumes she may inhale are bad for her.

Several very inexpensive blocks, like Banana Boat and No-Ad, get high marks for effectiveness, but they are made with active ingredients like retinyl palmitate, methylparaben, and oxybenzone that we would prefer not using on tiny tykes' skin. Blocks like Kiss My Face and Blue Lizard have no known endocrine disrupters or potential carcinogens, but their prices are much higher. There is no perfect solution to this dilemma, since this is stuff you should be slathering on your kids generously, making it tough on your wallet.

UV-PROTECTIVE CLOTHING

PROTECTIVE CLOTHING AND hats are a smart addition to wearing sunblock. Since the sun penetrates most clothing, you need to give some thought to what your kids wear. The darker the color, the tighter the weave, the more protection, but on a hot summer day you're inviting heatstroke. What's a smart mom to do?

- Invest in a few pieces of clothing with built-in UV protection and make sure one piece is a big floppy hat. The hip outdoorsy stores are well stocked and always have something on sale.
- Add "Sun Guard" to your wash to add UV protection to clothing for up to twenty washes. The only caveat: This is not recommended for babies under six months (https://sunguard sunprotection.com/faqs/info_6.html).

5

THE BABY WARDROBE

HE'S SO CUTE!

For one very brief moment in time, you're totally in charge of their sartorial finery. Feels good, right? Don't get used to it. In short order they'll be expressing their preference to wear the same tutu or torn tee daily (more on this in chapter seven). So don't let the fleeting power go to your head—never invest big bucks in any kid's clothing, particularly for a newborn. It's an investment with no return. Yes, it's easy to walk into Petite Bateau and get sucked in by the most charming miniature navy blue cardigan you've ever seen. It's easy to imagine how chic your little one will look with that cardigan over a fine blue-and-white pin-striped romper, teeny-tiny matching hat, and socks. Ah, *magnifique, bébé* . . . Can't you see yourself promenading them in their stroller, a big red balloon tied to the handle, passersby stopping to admire your smiling, cooing babe? Okay. You're allowed *one* ridiculous splurge.

After that, put it all on your baby registry list, and let others buy the stuff for you. Then return it and buy stuff your kid will really use. Or at least return all the teeny-tiny, impossibly adorable stuff everyone will buy (because it's so damned cute), and exchange them for bigger sizes. Get stuff your child will use when she's nine months or a year or two old, when you'll finally get how stupid it is to buy this stuff (yes, everyone is telling you, but we know you're not quite there yet). Trust us: By then you'll have gone broke on all the other baby necessities (diapers, nipples, breast pads—as satisfying as buying tires for a car) and you'll have lost the impulse to splurge on whatever designer Suri Cruise happens to be wearing. You'll be happy to have a few killer outfits in reserve for family pictures and special events.

BABY ENVY

LET'S GET THIS straight at the outset: The only celebrity baby you should be concerned with is your own. Why is our culture obsessed by overprivileged and overpromoted people hustling their products, their bodies, their surgically enhanced looks, and now their babies? What makes these "stars" baby experts? They're not. It's just the media looking for a way to sell their magazines and papers. It's just manufacturers looking for ways to hustle their goods. It's just celebs looking for ways to promote themselves by pimping their kids. Ugh.

Do not use celeb mamas as role models. You cannot afford their lifestyles—however seductive, slick, or gorgeous they seem. Forget about the moms with the perfectly toned bodies and Zen calm, photographed in front of marvelously healthy meals in pristine kitchens. They'll make you feel like you're doing something wrong when you have a sink piled with dishes, loads of laundry to be folded, and you're still struggling to fit back into your pre-maternity wear. Trust us, if you had a personal trainer, personal chef, full-time nanny, oh, and endless funds for clothes, you could look like them, too.

Once all the expensive adorableness is out of your system, go to Walmart, Target, Carter's, or online to Wayfair and buy prebundled packs of all-cotton white kimono T-shirts, onesies, and simple bibs for your newborn. Invest in packages of cloth diapers (these are a mother's best friend, and you'll use them for everything—from protecting your shoulders from spit-up to simple cleanups). Don't waste money on special diaper covers, burp cloths, etc. Not necessary.

Plenty of books and Web sites tell you what you "must" have in your house before the baby's born. What's the rush? You do not know how big your baby will be. You do not know how fast he will grow. You may have the kid who hates footsies and long sleeves. Beyond the basics, buy things as they *need* them, and head straight to the clearance racks in the stores. Bottom line: Keep it simple and wait to buy. If in doubt, you don't need it.

CLOTHING

At any given stage during the first year, you'll probably need:

- four to eight pants-and-shirt sets
- four to six rompers
- four to six one-piece footed outfits
- five to seven undershirts (one-piece long- or short-sleeved onesies with snaps at the crotch. Instead of enduring the over-the-head tussle, we like kimono style: easy on, easy off)
- two soft cardigans
- one snowsuit or winter bunting (for those unfortunates who live in a cold clime)
- two to four pairs of booties or socks

- four hats (you'll lose them, so it's good to have a couple of extras on hand)

And after the first year? You won't need our advice.

STUFF

- Bassinet, Moses basket, crib, or someplace soft and safe for the rug rat–in-training to sleep
- New car seat
- Newborn pacifiers
- Swaddle blankets, sheets
- Bouncy chair and/or swing (you don't *need* both)
- Sling (depending on baby's temperament, this may be critical)
- Foam pad—converts any waist-level dresser top/tabletop into a changing table
- Diapering stuff
- Gentle baby soap
- Baby nail file (easier than clippers)
- A rectal thermometer (get over it)
- Breast pads (you may also need a breast pump and lanolin for sore nipples)
- Phone number for lactation consultant (don't be shy; ask for help! If after a few days her advice isn't working, be smart and find a new consultant)
- Nursing/feeding pillow. Our money's on the firm, adjustable My Brest Friend (beats Boppy hands down)
- Nursing cover/shawl, if you're modest (we like Hooter Hiders, but their lovely bold patterns don't exactly

make you inconspicuous. A simple blanket will work just fine)

- A few bright-colored, dangly, noisemaking toys (check out Manhattan Toy's assortment)
- Books with striking images. Never too early for books.

THE BOOK ON BABY

REMEMBER WHEN WE said, "Say no to everything"? We lied. Never say no to books! When your kids are older, hand-me-down books are awesome. But get your baby her own new board books to chew on. . . .

The Classic Collection

Pat the Bunny

Goodnight Moon

The Little Engine That Could

The Very Hungry Caterpillar

The Runaway Bunny

The Cat in the Hat

The Lady with the Alligator Purse

Brown Bear Brown Bear, What Do You See?

Eloise

The Story of Ferdinand

The Snow Day

Whistle for Willie

PART 2

ARE YOU READY YET?
Dressing to Express Yourself—
or Someone Else

INTRODUCTION

We love clothes. We love fashion. We love jewelry. Makeup, not so much, but we respect you if you do. Shoe obsession? Naturally. But just because we're fans of fashion doesn't mean we're slaves to fashion, or that we actually buy everything we're attracted to—we're not that kind of girl. And just because it's our business to know the trends and to edit the good from the bad, well, this doesn't mean that we haven't made our mistakes. We *are* that kind of girl. We're risk takers.

We're also mamas.

The smartest mama understands fashion as an art form and sees clothing as a method of communication. She manages her family's dress code, budgets, and choices accordingly. She knows high, buys low. Just because she can appreciate a Jasper Johns or Salvador Dalí doesn't mean she's going to buy the original. Just because she loves Chloe and Miu Miu doesn't mean she's going to buy their goods at full retail.

Your job is to be your kid's model and guide in making

mindful apparel and accessories choices. You're the teacher helping them figure out a whole bunch of important stuff: value and
values, what they need, when they need it, appropriate choices
for different occasions, how to care for what they own, where
to shop, and what messages their choices are communicating—
wittingly and unwittingly.

Remember their dress and clothing choices are just another
form of expression. So as your kids learn, take risks, and experiment to find their voice and style, try to control yourself, please.

And you thought you just needed to run to Target and get
them stuff.

6

THE RIGHT FIT

UNIFORMLY DIFFERENT

Identity. Style. Community. Clothing is an expression of all of these things. There's a fine line to walk between originality and fitting in with the pack, and between being appropriately attired for the weather/event/culture and being way out in left field. Have you ever arrived in jeans and a tee for a dinner you thought casual, to find everyone else dressed to kill? Or traveled to a foreign country, bought something everyone was wearing, only to get home to realize there was no way that orange sari or gray pajama pant was ever seeing the light of day?

Try to remember what it's like to be a kid as you think about their clothes and clothing choices. They're navigating a country in turmoil. At odds with their changing bodies, struggling to break away and to be independent, while at the same time longing to be part of the pack. They're dressing to cover up, to announce who they are, and to fit in with their peers during a time when each day presents a kaleidoscope of shifting social cues. Just as they're trying on clothing that fits who they are, or might want to be, so are the natives around them. It's no wonder that their taste in clothing changes. It's no wonder that they want to wear what everyone else is wearing one day and want to express their independence the next.

How do you help them figure this out?

THE HOME MODEL

Do these words sound familiar? "Be yourself." "Make up your own mind." "Don't follow the pack." "Be original." "Just because everyone is doing it doesn't mean you should be, too."

Who are you kidding? It's not that simple. If you're uttering these words to your kids, that's okay—there's real truth to them. But you should *also* be talking about all the inner and outer forces that make these messages hard to put into practice. Balance these messages with real-life talk and real-life solutions.

Look, every mom hopes these words will inoculate her kids against a host of parental anxieties (beyond just what they are wearing): early drinking, drugs, sex, purple hair, tongue rings, nipple rings, God-knows-where-else rings.

Hello! Do you drink? Do you do drugs (Ambien, Ativan, Xanax)? Do you have sex? Do you color your hair? Have a cute little tattoo on your hip? Pierced ears, nose, belly button? Are you label smitten? Do you buy clothes to fit into your community?

They're watching.

Are you an aspiring poet spending hours crafting your devil-may-care look: long skirts, hoop earrings, and artfully arranged askew hair? Are you sporting a professional and slightly sexy look for the office: white collared shirts, high-waisted pencil skirts, and tall platform pumps? Are you keeping up with the gym divas: spinning, stretching, Zumba'ing in Lululemon, Athletica and Nike, despite their outrageous price tags?

They're watching.

You don't wear sweats to your job in the bank. You don't attend a PTA meeting in sequin short shorts. You dress up for a wedding. Wear black to a funeral.

They're watching.

As in all things, for better or worse, you are their first and most important role model. Your relationship with how you dress, what you wear, where you shop is their first cue. Know your own motivations as you go about getting dressed. Discuss the choices you make and why. (By the way, it is perfectly acceptable and healthy to posit "because it's to-die-for cute" as a reason. We're not judging. And remember, kids can sniff out lying from a mile away.)

Give them the latitude to make awful, ugly, weird, even unflattering choices in their clothing so they can find their own comfort zone and sense of style. At the same time, set boundaries: no jeans to their grandparents' fiftieth anniversary party because your in-laws will find it disrespectful (you don't need more of that grief), no buying your eight-year-old thong underwear emblazoned with a heart that reads, "I'm Ready."

In the end, what they wear is not all that important as long as mindful choices are being made. And yes, sometimes these choices have nothing to do with who they are, and everything to do with who they might like to be.

You do it, too. Get over it.

7

JOIN THE CLUB—
but Which One?

LABEL LUST

Snobby, slutty, PG, NC-17, highbrow, lowbrow, preppy, Goth, psychotic, normal, designer, glammy, regular, casual, Ivy League, conservative, liberal . . . all terms used to label: behavior, beliefs, styles, states of mind. The label is shorthand to identify and categorize. To create a kind of order out of chaos. Design a hierarchy. Figure out where things fit. Affix value to uncertainty.

We're all tempted to look to labels and brands as a marker of quality and taste. Yet the rise of the designer label has more to do with aspirational marketing than it does with high-quality product. Yes, there are brilliant designers and manufacturers who produce fantastic lines of product . . . say, for example, Hermès. Beautiful, stylish, well crafted, and unaffordable. But not all that glistens is gold.

TAG IT

Are you mesmerized when someone walks by wearing a polo shirt with a jumbo-size guy on horseback stretched across the bosom? How about shoes and jewelry encrusted with massive CCs? Do you think, *Ooh! Great style! I want that!* Or do you think, *Huh, that person paid a hefty price for the privilege of advertising for a company.* (Maybe a little of both?) Ask yourself: Do you really and truly want to hustle for Ralph Lauren, Chanel, Tommy Hilfiger? Do you really want to be a grown woman wearing an NFL or MLB or NHL jersey—player's name stitched on the back—when you're not at the game? Maybe you do! We're not judging (we swear!). What we *do* judge is obliviousness about what you're doing: shelling out big bucks to advertise for corporations that you probably don't even have stock in.

Teach your kids that just because an alligator is lounging on a polo shirt, or Coach initials run wild on a bag, it's no guarantee that the quality of the goods is superior. And help make them aware of the marketing strategy inherent in these items. If your kid wants to be a billboard and pay extra for it, that's fine and dandy. Hell, we all do this sometimes! Just be sure that when they're old enough for the lightbulb to go off over their heads, they're aware of how the world works.

THE MICKEY MOUSE CLUB: LOOK FOR THE CELEBRITY LABEL

As for so-called "celebrity" labels . . . Come on; think about it: Aren't they just a little goofy? Sure, little ones often wear Mickey Mouse or Dora the Explorer gear. But we're still scratching our heads as to why anyone would buy a Jessica Simpson shoe, dress, or trouser just because her name is slapped on the label.

And we must admit to being a little freaked out seeing Snooki on the cover of *Rolling Stone* and reading the article to find her aspirational goal is to be a brand like Jessica Simpson. (It's kind of like an alternate-merchandise-reality play within an alternate-merchandise-reality play.) We guess you can't blame her, though, since Jessica's apparel lines are closing in on a billion dollars in sales. Equally, we would run for the hills before heading to Kohl's for LC Lauren Conrad. And Bongo at Kmart by Audrina Patridge. Uh, why?

We hate to admit it, but we've done our homework, and some of the stuff is good, like the collaboration between Miley Cyrus and Max Azria (BCBG) for Walmart. Nice-looking, well priced. Hey, we think Shaun White is pretty cool and were excited to see his licensed products for boys at Target. Great looking, reasonably priced—and he's a way more interesting role model than, say, Britney Spears. (Just saying.) Look, we're not going to tell you not to buy Jessica's stuff or Miley's stuff or Selena Gomez's line for Kmart (also cute). But buy them only if you really like the look of the goods and their price points are similar to equally cute non-celebrity-endorsed duds. In short, we're bitchy (see our first book!), but we're not totally rigid, and you shouldn't be either.

Oh, one final note: We *are* rigid when it comes to baby and toddler clothes. . . . Sorry, but you may not spend an extra cent on a fancy logo for a child under four. Don't pimp your baby.

INFORM YOUR SPAWN

Teach your kids to think about what they're buying if they must have these goods. First of all, almost all of this stuff is produced via licensing agreements. The personalities, talented as they may be—or not be—are *not*, for the most part, fashion designers. They are selling their name, or Disney is selling their name, for a fee. (Typically licensing agreements pay back between 3 percent to 10 percent of wholesale sales.) So, for argument's sake, a Snooki tee (!) sold at retail for $25 ($12.50 at wholesale) could mean as much as $1.25 in her pocket. You feel like putting your hard-earned $1.25 in Snooki's pocket?

Let us remind you, it's not just Goofy's disciples playing this game. Sports teams have moved beyond just asking you to be a member of their nation by wearing a cap or jacket stamped with the team logo. They're asking you, your kids—even your pets— to wear apparel emblazoned with your favorite player's name. When you don a Jeter top, or your son wears Manning sweats, or Fido dresses in his Dale Earnhardt Jr. coat, just remember you're paying an upcharge for the privilege of letting them win your hard-earned bucks.

THE BROTHERHOOD OF SAGGING PANTS AND THE SISTERHOOD OF (OH, MY!) NO PANTS

Before you had kids, you saw boys jumping on the subway in the city or cruising the streets in suburbia wearing pants that sagged. As waistbands inched toward their thighs, boxers and cracks exposed, you couldn't help but be fascinated about the tipping point. Which move or misstep meant the pants would fall down to their ankles? Were their shorts glued to their pants—or sewn on? It reminded you of when the elastic had gone in your panty hose and you could feel them crawling down below your pelvis, settling onto your hips. . . . You moved gingerly, hoping they wouldn't end up around your ankles. You felt for these boys with the sagging pants. So much work keeping them up. Of course, you also thought, *How ridiculous. If I have a kid there is no way he's wearing pants like that.*

When Gaga went gaga with the no-pants look, and Rihanna copied her, and Madonna (how old is she?) joined in, you thought, *Why would anyone want to walk out the door in their bathing suit unless they're going to the beach? How silly is this?! I'm not exposing my thighs and bottom.* Your daughter heading out the door in what is essentially a leotard and tights to anything but ballet? Never.

Being a mom is humbling. Isn't it? Now Tony has joined the brotherhood and Maria the sisterhood, what's a mom to do?

It's wise to be honest. Expressing how you feel about their looks is within bounds, as long as you can maintain a reasoned discussion. Ask them questions about what they like about the look. Educate yourself—and them. Does Tony know that the sagging-pants look was started in prison by men advertising their availability? Is Maria sure she wants to go pantless, when copying her idol's fashion statement is also sending out a sexualized message? Still, let them experiment. Consider putting safe boundaries on the places where they can dress in what may be provocative attire. When they are still young, you'll have some control. As they get older, unless you think there is more going on (like Tony is joining the Sharks and Maria is putting her exposed bum in harm's way), there is not much you can do but grin and bare—er, bear it.

THE DAUGHTER OF THE FLOUNCY TRIPLE-TIER DRESS

FOR ONE WHOLE year, our youngest insisted on dressing as a princess-cowgirl (not the Disney kind of princess, but a home-grown kind). It was a bit of a puzzle. Despite a varied ward-robe, she insisted on wearing the same long blue sleeveless dress, cowboy boots, and a sparkly hair tie to school. Every single day. In the beginning, we tried to convince her that the dress was for birthday parties, not a messy, busy school day. She would not budge. We urged her to wear sneakers on the playground. She refused. Winter came, and we offered up other flouncy skirts and warm sweaters. "No!" was her only answer. We let her be.

The dress and those boots are now put away in a clothing bag labeled, "Posterity," and, as much as any picture or journal, they are a part of her history. She went on to develop a keen fashion eye, even working one summer in Bloomingdale's executive training program while she was trying on a career in retail.

Our point: Let them find their way. No harm, and, as long as the washer and dryer work, no foul.

Just remember: Clothing is a form of nonverbal communication announcing gang membership, social status or wannabe social status, hipness, squareness, green-ness, preppiness, jocki-ness, defiance—and they're trying them all on. Let them express themselves; it's part of their development.

8

WHAT THEY NEED, WHERE TO GET IT:
The Basics and Beyond

Are you one of those moms who make a clothing list for each child at the beginning of each season and stick to it? Brava! We can't. (That admission's a bit of an embarrassment, but we're honest.) That said, we're really good at making an inventory of needs by child, even if we don't religiously follow it. Once your kids have acquired goods (whether begged, bought, or borrowed), it's complicated to sort through the debris to see what they need. Whether their drawers are overflowing or they have an unholy attachment to one shredded graphic tee, it's messy and confusing.

So, to help you figure this out, we're sharing our simple clean-out inventory-and-assessment process. (If you're an OCD neatnik, skip this section; we're sure you've got this covered.)

THE DUMP OF NO RETURN

Before you know it, they're no longer tots and have strong opinions about what they're wearing—and they want *more, more, more*. Their drawers are crammed full, overflowing with last year's/this year's/next year's wardrobe (not to mention the bags of hand-me-downs from the older cousins filling the attic). The stuff builds up fast—and yet despite the sheer abundance, they say they need more. Huh? Here's how we approach the madness:

STEP 1: Start by putting a nice bottle of sauvignon blanc in the fridge.

STEP 2: Lasso your kid. This is their stuff. They must help. They must also get a say in what stays, what goes, and what they need.

STEP 3: Remove *everything* from their closets and drawers, and pile it on their beds. Why bed? Because in order for them to go to sleep, you'll need to have sorted, purged, and put everything away.

STEP 4: Set up and label brown paper bags: keepers, goods in negotiation, charity, swap, consignment, eBay, yard sale, hand-me-down, cedar closet, save for posterity, etc.

STEP 5: Classify and categorize all clothing into separate piles: long-sleeved and short-sleeved shirts, T-shirts, underwear, socks, jeans, trousers, skirts, dresses, shoes, boots, shorts, sweaters, etc.

STEP 6: Then break everything down by color, season, and weight.

STEP 7: Separate what fits from what doesn't. Put garments that still fit but that your child refuses to wear into the "negotiation" basket. (As for the ones you wish they wouldn't wear, control yourself.)

STEP 8: Remove what is no longer worn, decide on dispensation, and toss into labeled bags. Inventory what is left.

STEP 9: Start the list: The cute Gap yellow-and-green calico skirt still fits, but the polo jersey that went with it didn't make the cut. Put a new green top on the list. Daryl has stretched like an *X-Men* mutant and his arms and legs poke out of the long pants and shirts, but tees and shorts still fit. Add pants and long-sleeved shirts. Once-white Champion athletic socks (those that have not been digested by the dryer monster) are a disgrace. New athletic socks for everyone.

STEP 10: Tuck them into bed and pour yourself a nice glass of chilled wine. You'll need it.

We'll be honest: As our kids aged and their apparel inventory increased, we would become a little unhinged (okay, full disclosure—a lot unhinged) when we found buried away, forgotten, or pricey "this-will-make-me-happy-forever-and-you-will-never-need-to-buy-me-another-thing-as-long-as-we-both-shall-live" things crumpled in the back of drawers or forgotten on the closet floor.

Try to be a better mom than we were. Your job is to model how to manage the things they own, how to assess what stays and goes, and help them figure out what they need. Honor their taste, judgments, and preferences. So if they're attached to a cringe-worthy romper or a number 85 Ochocinco tee—keep your feelings to yourself. Remember the wine is in the chiller.

MAKE IT FUN

CRANK UP THE music and make the purge festive. Cook cookies, pop popcorn. Stage a fashion hall of shame walk for the worst of the worst in their closets. Dress them up. Dress up their dolls. Dress up the dog. Take campy photos you can laugh about one day. (Caution: When you go to sell on eBay, *never, ever* post pictures of the kids online. Photograph the garments separately.)

ECO-NOMIZE

Now it's time to tackle the pile of rejects and outgrown goods.

Teach your kids to be good citizens of earth. Teach them that things don't just appear and disappear. Reuse and repurpose all of their possessions, and make them help. Bring kids to the consignment shop or charity dropoff, or have them help you post on eBay or thredUP. Think of this as part of their education, like visiting a farm to appreciate what goes into the food you eat or going to a dump that requires strict sorting of refuse. Make them more conscious consumers.

JUST THE BASICS

YOU'D BE SURPRISED how many questions we get about what a basic kids' wardrobe should look like. To give you a jumping-off point (and ammunition in the battle of "but everyone has eight different sweaters in shades of yellow"), we've created a bare-bones basic list for what they should have in their closet. Of course, this will vary depending on local conditions and personalities, like if your child wears school uniforms, or only sweats, or you've got a girly-girl who shuns pants.

three to four pairs of jeans or school pants

two to three pairs of sweat- or yoga pants

six to seven school shirts

two to three sweatshirts/hoodies

two to three seasonal sweaters

two to three pairs of pj's

six to seven T-shirts (assorted/graphic/white/simple)

seven to ten pairs of underwear

seven pairs of socks

three pairs of tights

two swimsuits

one pair of dress shoes

one pair of athletic shoes

one pair of rain boots

one pair of winter boots (if needed)

flip-flops

two to three skirts

two "dressy dresses"

one sport jacket

one pair of dress slacks or khakis

three pairs of shorts

> one winter coat/snow pants/mittens/hat/scarf
>
> one light spring/fall coat
>
> one rain slicker

OUT IN THE WORLD

Now you're ready to go shopping. Your mission? To stay on budget, clothe your kids, and teach them how to manage the retail cycle all on their own. Clever buyers mix up their purchases between big-box retailers, small shops, online sites, and thrift and consignment shops. Know when it's the season to buy and be on the hunt for items at value pricing. Smart mamas do not invest in expensive kids' clothing or overspend on special-occasion clothing. Taking advantage of thrift, consignment, and swapping of used and gently worn kids' clothing is eco-conscious and wise. Finally, the smartest of mamas separates herself from her child and doesn't overspend to compensate for what she wishes she had.

DAMN YOU, AL GORE, FOR INVENTING THE INTERNET

Once upon a time, home entertainment was a straightforward three-network-and-PBS event; the morning paper arrived at the door with all the news fit to print; the travel agent booked airline and hotel reservations; and books were distributed to local bookstores by publishers. Shopping for clothes, too, used to be a simpler task.

A merchant bought goods from a manufacturer and put them out on the floor for sale (not "on sale"—*for* sale). You'd scope out the latest fashions by looking at the ads in the Sunday paper or in magazines, or view them in the stores when you went for back-to-school or Easter shopping. Whether it was a discount store, a department store, an off-price store, or a local specialty store, you'd walk in, touch the goods, try them on, and buy them.

Today, the Internet has thrown retail pricing and distribution for a loop. From high-fashion designers like Carolina Herrera and Thakoon preselling fresh-off-the-runway styles online through sites like modaoperandi.com, to individual craftspeople making and selling on Etsy, to the "flash sale mob," how you buy, where you buy, when you buy, and from whom you buy are changing at breakneck speed.

Everyone has an online presence. Big and small makers are cutting out the middle guy. With the advent of flash sale sites, even the middle guy doesn't look like your mother's middle guy anymore. Discounts and bargains abound. It's often hard to distinguish between good and bad sites, worthy and unworthy vendors. For a careful consumer, information and option overload can feel like a burden. Should I buy this now? Which smartphone app is the most up-to-date for instant price comparison? Should I go home and do more research? I'm sure I can find the same thing for less with a little more clever Googling. Wait, I've found it for less, but I've never heard of this Web site. Is it safe? Is shipping free both ways? What about returns?

Look, you're busy. Time is money. You can drive yourself insane looking for the "best" deal. We think when it comes to kids' clothing and accessories it's wisest to think convenient, cheap, simple. When they're small and before they want to express themselves, before they balk at castoffs, grab those hand-me-downs, think thrift shops, and run for the corner consignment. Then fill in purchases at big-box stores.

The big-box retailers do an outstanding job of meeting the needs of growing kids. They are trend right and well priced, they stand behind their products, and they are convenient to shop—

online or in person. That said, a mama has to be savvy. Insist on fair value and fair pricing. Don't shop at stores that consistently place goods on the floor at inflated prices just so they can turn around a few weeks later and offer them to you at a so-called "special promotion" or "sale" price.

A MAMA'S FIRST STOPS

WHETHER ONLINE OR in person, the first destination should be clearance and sales racks. Think of it this way: Once upon a time your spouse or mate was young, appealing, attractive; you couldn't wait to make them your own. Now you've had 'em around for a while, and maybe some of the ecstasy has faded, but the love and comfort remain. Same goes for items now on the clearance racks. They were a lot sexier when they were fresh and merchandised at the front together with all the new goods. But trust us: Once you get them home they'll wear just fine.

THE DEPENDABLES: TARGET AND WALMART

Fact is, you can buy everything you need at Target or Walmart, or both, and have a pretty cute-looking kid for not a lot of dough. When our kids were little, we sort of lived at Target. What we like is that we can get in and out and check off the list: T-shirts, jeans, pajamas, underwear, socks, flip-flops, Converse All Stars. And while we still head to see what's on sale, you don't need to wait for the merch to get marked down, because it's fairly priced and usually well stocked.

BABY DUDS

HOPEFULLY YOU WON'T need to buy clothes for the new baby. You've got all those baby gifts, and you *are* going to accept any and all hand-me-downs (no snobbery allowed!) while they can't put up a fight. If you need to fill out the wardrobe, Target is a terrific option. Their Circo line is basic, well made, affordable. (We like their infant cotton "yoga pants"—a dead ringer for the pricier ones from that hipster paradise, American Apparel.) Old Navy, the Children's Place, Carter's, and H&M are good sources for basics, too, and we've also had terrific luck at local kids' consignment stores.

We admit it: Nothing reads "sweet fresh baby" like a Hanna Andersson wide-striped onesie with a little knit cap, but please skip the matching mama outfit. Baby Gap? Not worth it.

OLD NAVY

For being trendy, fashion-forward, cute . . . almost no one gets it done as cost-effectively as Old Navy. Remember we talked about taking a risk as being part of our fashion philosophy? Go here for cost-effective risks. When Kat, the most popular girl in third grade, arrives at school sporting the latest chic tweener gear and your little Kitty comes home roaring to follow, head over to Old Navy—the price is right.

THE GAP

We like what we see at GapKid. The quality is a cut above their sister merchant (Old Navy), and the looks are great from everyday basic to fashion forward, but we struggle with their pricing. So, unless you're in a pinch, buy here only on sale.

H&M AND ZARA

Cool go-to destinations for the hipster mom and her kids. Well priced and reasonably well made. Find funky mini faux-leather bomber jackets, cool hats, distressed jeans. We've found tweener-sized blazers at Zara for under $30 that even the fashionista Olsen twins would be proud to sport. And we happen to be acquainted with one newly potty-trained toddler who proudly sports H&M's monster-truck Euro-style undies. Work it, baby.

PRO-CHOICE ON A BUDGET

STOP BEING A complete control freak when you go shopping. Remember to:

- let them experiment
- let them select their own clothes
- let them look ridiculous and make mistakes

You need to be organized. You've already figured out what the kiddos need; now budget accordingly before you begin a shopping excursion. As they get older, include them in the budget process. It's a good idea to let them know what the budget is for their seasonal wardrobes (it's a good idea for you to know, too!). This is both a teaching tool and an antistruggle tool as they whine and wheedle, pleading for the baseball shirt or fuzzy vest that will make their life complete but bust your bank.

By middle school, it's a good idea to give them discretionary clothing dollars and let them manage pieces of their wardrobe. Start with an allowance for accessories (if they mess up, they'll still be clothed), and go from there. Let them make choices that they'll have to live with, good and bad. Plus, they won't be able to blame you for having "nothing to wear" when they decide they don't like the black-and-white-plaid harem pants five weeks after they were purchased.

(continued)

While they'll still go with you, bring them shopping. Make them try the clothes on before you leave the store. No back-and-forth shopping and returning if they don't fit or pass muster. As kids get older, they'll want to be dropped off at the mall or in the town center. We're all for working toward a seasonal clothing allowance and letting them run with it. Be strong.

L.L.BEAN

Have a long line of rug rats in your family? Consider L.L.Bean. This outfit has expanded in recent years, bringing their clothing and rugged brand of outerwear and footwear out of Freeport, Maine, to more locations in the United States. Their brick-and-mortar reach is limited, and our one big issue with this great merchant is that it doesn't offer everyday free shipping both ways. (As of this writing, they've just begun free shipping one way.) As a result, we struggled about whether to recommend Bean, but the following story (see box below) has stuck with us big-time . . . and we do love our old Bean rain boots, *and* our kids wore Bean jackets that were passed down through many families.

Plus, Bean is a surefire place to find superwarm, high-quality baby/toddler rain/snow gear. Yep, a little pricey, but if you live in a cold or wet clime, it's worth it to know your little bundle of blubbery joy won't get chilly tootsies. If you see Bean's baby stuff at the thrift store, lunge for it. You can trust the quality.

THE JACKET AND THE BEAN STOCK

OUR FRIEND TOLD us this story of his leather jacket. Many, many years ago when his kids were small (in age) and he was small (in size), he bought a leather aviator jacket from L.L.Bean. For years and years he wore it until it was worn soft and comfy as only a great leather jacket can become. But as his kids grew, he grew, too, and his favorite jacket ended up in the back of his closet. He couldn't easily zip it closed.

Over the last year he's been our hero for diligently and sanely losing weight. He cut back on portion sizes, takes his time eating, consumes mostly whole grains and veggies with meat only as a side dish, and is thoughtful about exercising.

Recently he pulled out the old L.L.Bean jacket from the back of his closet and it fit. This time he couldn't zip it, not because it was too tight, but because the zipper was broken. He brought it back to the store to see whether it could be repaired. A lovely clerk informed him they no longer repair zippers, but they always stand behind their products, and replaced it with a brand-new $350-plus leather jacket.

CREW CUTS NEED A SHAVE

Kids' clothes from J.Crew, particularly for your little man, are to-die-for adorable. C'mon, what hip mama wouldn't want to send the boy out in an Italian mini chino blazer ($148) worn over the cutest two-tone checked violet shirt ($85), tucked into perfectly worn-in Levi's 503s ($108). But unless you're the mother of eight or have found the perfect neighborhood resale shop guaranteed to return 80 percent on the original investment, spending that kind of money—no matter how cute he looks—is loco. So while we recommend J.Crew for mom's wardrobe (for style at a price), their little-people's duds can be purchased only when the store has had a major pricing crew cut.

CLAIRE'S

Little thrills can make big and little girls happy. Walmart is the world's largest jewelry purveyor. Target has a great costume jewelry and accessories area. Hey, even CVS and Walgreens sell the junk. But Claire's is the go-to bazaar for everything from wide leopard headbands, butterfly clips, and bib necklaces to rocker chains and crocheted cuffs. It's cheap. It's stylish. It's fun.

PACSUN

Surf's up, and we like this as a go-to shop for boys and girls. Truth be told, this is one of the few mall shops aimed at tweens, teens, and young adults that we don't have the urge to flee. Reliable brands with an ageless SoCal vibe, so you can always find something to make them happy. Buy from the clearance racks, where you'll find the same stuff in slightly different form. A tiered button-front dress is a tiered button-front dress, whether polka dot or plaid, and cargo shorts are cargo shorts, khaki or print. You're sure to find something on sale.

TWEEN HUSTLERS

As your kids get older and are influenced by the media and their friends, invest in earplugs and blinders. Stores like Abercrombie, Hollister, Gilly Hicks, and Victoria's Secret will be on their shopping list. The clothing is sharp, trendy, fashionable. But their trafficking in overly sexualized messages as a means to market their goods is ugly. Really ugly. Can you resist this? Probably not. Try, though. The reality is that most girls and boys will go to these places, whether you like it or not. What you *can* do is educate them; help make them mindful shoppers. More on this later.

IS THERE ANYTHING COSTCO ISN'T GOOD AT?

In our book, Costco is the best high-quality, priced-right merchant in the country. We're mad Costco shoppers, buying all our paper goods, lots of our groceries, and many household products there. We always keep an eye out for good apparel opportunities, too. We don't recommend a special trip in the hopes of filling in all your little person's personal needs, but keep a sharp eye out for athletic socks, underwear, sweats, tanks, jeans, pajamas, and seasonal offerings like swimwear and outerwear.

DEPARTMENT STORES

We *almost* never shop at department stores. We have our favorite very high-end drool emporiums (Barneys, Bergdorf, Neiman) where we employ our "search and lust" strategy and wait for the final end-of-season 60-to-70-percent-off sales to pounce on killer investment-grade pieces (this year a pair of Costume National boots, OMG—but we digress). And we have a hard-to-fit-shoe offspring—adult size five—and head to Nordstrom as a store of last and merciful resort to buy hard-to-find shoes. Other than that, we pass. Frankly, we find going into Kohl's and Macy's depressing. A rehashing of overpriced, overlicensed designer labels makes them a yawn. But they are committed to kids and juniors—so if it works for you, great. Just beware of their pricing schemes. High and low. Constant sales (see below). Even we can't figure it all out. We'd just as soon head over to Forever 21 or H&M for fast budget-right fashion.

OFF-PRICE RETAILERS

Yes, we know there are people who swear by them. Not us. Today's off-price channels (T.J.Maxx, Marshall's, Ross, etc.) really bug us. While they are still picking up deals from overruns, canceled orders, and end-of-season clearance from "full-price" retailers, a lot of their merchandise is manufactured and bought to go directly on their floors. We worked as a buyer at Filene's when the original Filene's Basement was just that: the basement of the store. Goods that couldn't be sold were cleared out to the basement for automatic markdown. It was amazing. The price tickets were stamped with the date the item came to the basement; after twelve days the basement price would be marked down by 25 percent, after eighteen days by 50 percent, after twenty-four days by 75 percent, and after thirty days, if not sold, the item would go to charity. People would come and hide the things they wanted to buy, hoping to purchase them after twenty-four days. A chemise in ladies might end up buried under a men's suit jacket, shoes from kids under a jewelry table; handbags might be found in hosiery bins. It was great! The merchandise was the real deal. Designer ball gowns from the original (and in those days only) Neiman Marcus in Dallas. Chanel bags from I. Magnin. Shoes from Delman salon at Bergdorf.

Ah! The good old days.

Shop the big off-price stores knowing the good old days are long gone. Snooping around and weeding through the inventory, we've occasionally found good deals on lingerie, pajamas, and designer-label jeans.

Sadly, our heart no longer races.

ALWAYS THINKING LOCAL

OUR FIRST INSTINCT is to support a local store. Neighborhood children's shops are like the printed book—an endangered species. If you have one in your community and you like the owners (for years we tried to support our local toy store, only to finally give up when we decided the owner was a nasty curmudgeon who hated kids) and their pricing is in the ballpark, go there: Support your local store.

9

WHEN TO BUY:
Just in Time

For adults, we advise shopping for great deals: Cruise the stores, identify the must-haves, watch and wait, and pounce on markdowns at the end of each season (see our first book, *Bitches on a Budget*). We don't recommend this as a strategy for growing kids, except for things like hats, mittens, socks, maybe underwear and pajamas. Anything else and you run the risk of stockpiling and hoarding, only to come out way behind in the dollar game for two reasons: It's impossible to predict their physical growth, and it's impossible to predict what the "look" will be at school.

We offer this advice instead: Before kids start a new grade or a new school, head out and find a few new outfits that they love. Just like you'd want to look and feel your best the first week at a new job, so does your kid. We can talk loving yourself and having core strength and self-esteem, but face it: First impressions and how you feel about yourself matter.

Then wait. Sit on more clothing purchases. Unless your kids

are style casters or completely oblivious, don't buy their entire new wardrobe before school starts. Get the basics done. Let them get the lay of the land. See what the social norms are. Wait a bit; then finish out their wardrobes. It will save you big bucks two ways: You'll hit some good clearance sales after school starts, and the kids will be more likely to wear the clothes they buy.

WAIT. WAIT. DON'T TELL ME: IS IT CLEARANCE? IS IT A SALE? IS IT A SPECIAL OFFER?

No one can take issue with a fair exchange of money for goods or services. After all, every business needs to make a profit, or else they won't be able to pay employees, pay rents, pay taxes, stay open. Retailers are no different. They, too, need to make a buck or they won't be able to stay in business. We have no problem with this.

But we *do* have issues with sellers that jack up margins, inflating the price of a product just to turn around and mark the item down so they can promote discounts.

How does this work? Let's say a store buys a T-shirt for $6 that it would normally sell for $12. But since consumers are trained to buy on sale, the store puts the T-shirts out on the floor at a price of $15 for, say, six weeks. (There are laws that govern the amount of time goods need to be on the floor or available for purchase before a retailer can mark an item down and call it a sale.) Maybe they'll sell some at that $15 price, which is great for them, but their real aim is to then offer those T-shirts on "promotion" for $12, which is what they really planned all along.

How can you tell? If you see lots and lots of an item on display, say cashmere sweaters, available in every size and every imaginable color and on "special promotion," chances are they were bought for just this reason. On the other hand, on occasion a retailer does guess wrong and makes a big investment in something that never quite caught on—jumpsuits, anyone?—or the weather is unseasonable, leaving a full run of winter coats or swimsuits to clear out.

So if you've taken our advice and waited to purchase, once school is in session or once Easter has come and gone you'll be finding some pretty sweet real clearance items. The rule of retail is that old goods must make way for new goods, and the way stores do that is by marking down and clearing out items that haven't sold. We're at our shopping best buying clearance-style markdowns.

HURRY. HURRY. CLICK AND GET IT: FLASH SALE MOBS AND THE POWER OF THE GROUP

Before we enter the Wild West of online retailing, we want to caution you to hold on to your wallets, zip your purses, and control yourself. These guys depend on creating a running-of-the-brides atmosphere to get you to click and buy in a hurry. This is for adults only. If you can't control yourself, you may not enter. These are our rules: Do not buy something you are not in the market for. Do not buy something that you cannot return unless you are certain it is exactly what you were looking for. Do not buy a service or a restaurant certificate because it "sounds" good online. Read the fine print. Prior knowledge, desire, and careful reading of the offer are required before you are allowed to make a purchase. Okay. Now that you know the rules you may enter.

Gilt Groupe, Rue La La, Ideeli, and One Kings Lane (the flash retail mob), and Groupon, Living Social, Mamapedia ("the groupies") are among the original big players in the online-flash-sale and group-discount-purchase game. Companies entering the online mixed-media retail arena multiply daily, with the Internet's big gorilla, Google, the latest to test the waters. The business model continues to mutate (for example, Gilt Groupe and Rue are offering services and travel deals, even perishable foods, in addition to apparel and home goods), making it almost impossible to keep up with the sites and their seemingly endless product offerings.

The flash sale mobs specialize in selling discounted manufacturer overstocks and goods made for them in limited quantities and in a limited time frame—usually thirty-six to forty-eight hours. We offer mixed reviews.

We've successfully bought things like Ray-Ban Wayfarer sunglasses and a trash bin at good prices, but we've found inflated original retail pricing comparatives more than once. This makes us suspicious. We've also found products we've never heard of and have a hard time finding online. How does one ascribe a savings to a product that doesn't appear to have a "real" market value? The good news is that you're sitting at your computer, so if you do find something that's a must, put it into your cart (usually you have ten minutes to decide) and get your fingers busy seeing whether you can find the same item elsewhere at reputable stores to get a measure of the real market price. Better yet, since you're minding your budget, put it in your cart and let the time expire.

Groupon, Living Social, and Google are among a cast of seemingly thousands offering online daily group deals and discounts on everything from local ballet classes to shawarma and falafel to car seats. Click with caution.

Make sure what you're buying is something you actually were looking for and needed. The biggest problem with these sites isn't the deal (although a lot of the stuff is pretty awful); it's that you end up with unbudgeted things you really don't want or need. Clench your fists (you won't be able to use that clicking finger) and try to tune them out.

A CAUTIONARY TALE

OF COURSE WE'RE savvy enough not to bite on the massage being offered by Dan's Teeth Whitening, Botox, Spa, and Grooming Salon. You know, the one-stop, fill-'er-up, bleach-'em-and-wash-the-dog place in a town you passed once on the highway. But when we saw a deal for 60 percent off a massage at a place that was just a block away, we clicked. (Hey, we were stressed out, the deadline for this manuscript a week away.) Well, we didn't get past taking our shoes off before we decided there were better ways to get bedbugs or be seen on a live-streaming Girls Girls Girls video in some creep's basement. Awkwardly, we made some excuse about a forgotten pot of soup on the stove and fled. Our bargain cost us, big-time.

Remember, you do not need a dedicated daily e-mail for hot tot stuff. If you can't control the temptation for cute merch your kid doesn't need and your pocketbook can't afford—unsubscribe.

10

FANCY PANTS:
The Dance, Prom, Bar Mitzvah, Wedding Circuit

Rosie is twelve and suddenly on the circuit. Every third weekend there's a school or church dance, a bar or bat mitzvah, a birthday bash or holiday party. Her social life eclipsed yours long ago, but now there is an added note of pageantry, preening, and primping. Not only does she want to go for a mani-pedi before a big event and get her tresses washed, blown flat, ironed, or curled, she also wants a new dress for each and every occasion.

This is the time for her to become secondhand Rosie. Unless it's *her* bat mitzvah or confirmation, or she's the maid of honor at your next wedding, you may not indulge her. It's easy to get caught up in her enthusiasm. After all, you have no life, and, despite our warnings, you're living vicariously through her (see Part VI, "The Whole Child"). What mom doesn't want her kid to have everything? Stop. Take a deep breath, zip your lips and purse, and make this fun.

GLAMOUR WEAR

With so many great inexpensive clothing options, there's no need to spend hundreds and hundreds of dollars on fancy kiddie dresses or suits. You don't need to go to pricey department or specialty stores. These are *kids'* clothes. Obsolescence is on its way before you know it, between their outgrowing them and changing their minds.

Do not go online to the shops that sell dresses for proms. The dresses are outrageously pricey and often not returnable. *This* is the time to troll eBay, Goodwill, the Salvation Army. Head over to the local kids' consignment shops (beware—check pricing before buying; these are not always the bargain you might believe). Visit Zara, Forever 21, and H&M. Organize a neighborhood swap. Encourage your kids to trade.

Be a beggar. Be a collector. Hoard. Or at the very least be the eager recipient of older kids' outgrown party wear. Put them in bags and haul them out when the time comes. We did this with our kids; gems and dogs came out of the bags. Some of the stuff was just ugly (expensive but ugly), other things horribly dated— like a long navy velvet puffy-sleeved dress with a high lace collar for a fourteen-year-old. Still others were really cute. The amazing thing about all the fancy-pants loot was that every single garment, no matter who had handed it on, was in pristine condition. Don't spend a lot of money on this stuff. Let your friends do that.

LET YOUR HAIR DOWN

WHILE WE CAUTIONED against their high prices, J.Crew's Crew-cuts does have a broad line of fantastic skirts for girls, and these are the kinds of pieces to pick up on sale and have on hand for a special occasion. Perfect for dressing up and dressing down. Available in children's to preteens' sizing. Black, blue, gold, layered, ruffled, shirred—all you need to do is match with a dressy top and cute shoes and they're ready for a party, or add a T-shirt and boots for dinner or school. We love the versatility of these pieces: a grape juice spill on top doesn't mean the party outfit ends up in the discard pile—just change out the shirt; they fit all sizes and body types; and with elastic-banded waists they can last more than one season.

MIRACLE WORKER

This is also the time to begin to teach your daughter about the miracle of a little basic dress. Changing it up with accessories like necklaces, belts, boas, scarves, or capes makes a single dress go a long way. Or show her how versatile a cute frilly black skirt can be—dressed up or down with great tops and tees, dressy shoes, or hiker boots. And, not to be sexist in the preening department: It's also the time to show your son how a different color and texture shirt, tie, vest, or sweater can liven up a basic blazer.

KEEPING THEM IN THE RIGHT AGE

WHEN OUR KIDS were little, an acquaintance recounted the story of her son's end-of-year school dance. All the kids were required to wear formal wear. Her son was in a jacket and tie. He bought a corsage for his date. A limousine picked them up from her house (she showed us the pictures) and took the group to a dance, took them out to dinner, and brought them back to her house for an after-party. We listened with a plastered smile, nodding in all the right places, cooing about how adorable her son and his date looked.

The kids were in fifth grade.

Not to sound like your mom or anything, but they grow up fast enough. Unless you're part of the landed gentry and the hunt goes through on the weekends, unless your downtown club requires jackets and ties on the young men and dresses on the young ladies, get with the program. It's 2012, not 1912. Save your money and preserve your values.

GROOM THE PARTY

Prom and party preening can cost big bucks. Draw the line. No salon visits. No pricey mani-pedis. Help her organize a gathering at your house before the big event, complete with full grooming services (the girls can do one another's hair and nails). Swing by the local beauty-supply store and stock up on a bunch of nail polish and hair products. Buy Sally Hansen appliqués at CVS. Ask an "expert" makeup artist to come (don't you have a friend who's really good at applying eyeliner?), or show the girls some age-appropriate instructional YouTube videos about hair, nails, makeup. This is an opportunity to teach kids how to enhance without going over-the-top.

11

THE SHOE THING

As we were writing this book, we asked our Facebook fans about basic needs and how many clothes they own. The responses to our question confirmed that most of us are human. Few in our budget-conscious, careful-spender audience said they stuck to necessities. But the one item that blew their clothing budget wide-open? Shoes. No surprise, really—our audience is 95 percent women. What was a surprise was the number of pairs in their *kids'* wardrobes.

A DIGRESSION:
Why Do Women Love Shoes?

THIS GOT US to thinking about shoes and why we love them. Why is it we have so many pairs and they are all so different? (One might argue that the twelve pairs of black heels in our closet are all the same, but they'd be missing their complex nuances: the slightly different heel heights, subtly different toe caps, variations in leather grain.)

Recently while traveling we were walking and window-shopping. The complex architecture of the latest platform shoes caught our eye, and we spent considerable time calculating where our center of gravity would reside. Would we topple over in them? Surely we'd be hobbled like an ancient bound-footed Chinese woman. Haven't women come farther than this? We passed by.

We didn't get but two blocks before we were stopped dead in our tracks by the most stunning, simple, elegant over-the-knee black boot. Perfect. Tall, lean, aristocratic. At once soft, supple, hard, and stately. Best of all, this boot had a long zipper up the back. It was the sexiest article of clothing we had ever seen. Ever. We wanted to stop and make them ours. Yes, we may be on a budget, but this fell into our splurge-worthy category if any item in the history of time ever did. But we were running late for a date and marched on.

We left town the next day and had no time to run back to the shop.

This experience left us wondering: What is it about shoes? Do they mirror our innermost fantasies? Are they ready-made embodiments of our various identities? Work boots, hikers, peep-toes, ballet shoes, stilettos, oxfords, flats, Keds. Perhaps they're each simply a reflection of the complexity of every modern woman—wife, mother, sister, daughter, party girl, lover, worker, power broker, on and on. No other accessory can so entirely embody and transform and ground (fleetingly) our self-conception.

IF THE SHOE FITS

We're big fans of having growing feet measured and fitted for one pair of all-purpose, everyday shoes: athletic shoes, oxfords— whatever. This is one of those times we go to the local store that's been in business for generations and specializes in taking care of precious growing tootsies. As for flip-flops, ballet flats, boots, etc., the big-box guys do a damn fine job of staying on trend at rock-bottom pricing. Our other destination for shoes is factory outlet stores. We'll go on record here as saying that while you're not always getting the biggest bargain in the world at these stores (because they, too, are selling goods manufactured for this line of distribution, in addition to true clearance), you almost always find a deep assortment of products. Since time is money and dragging kids around can be a drag, in our book more is better, and outlets have lots and lots of stuff. As for online bargain and overstock sites, take a pass unless the shipping is free both ways.

ZAPPOS IS STILL THE BEST

Zappos is the best online retailer we've ever done business with. Period. Great service. Huge assortments. Reasonable (not the cheapest—but fair) pricing. Order online and the goods seem to appear overnight. Too small? Too big? Not what you bargained for? Send them back for free—you have up to one year to return unworn shoes for full price. Come on; does it get better?

OH, NO! BABY SHOES

WHEN WAS THE last time you saw an infant running around? Why would you buy sandals for them? And does a toddler need $200 designer shoes? Your little ones have plenty of time to develop their own shoe fetish; do not impose yours on them. If you're thinking of tootsie coverings for a prewalker, think cheap, think warm, think things that don't fall off!

12

OLD STYLE RENEWAL

Maybe you're the mom with a little hipster darling. Without direction, she repurposes and wears her big brother's castoff lumberjack red flannel shirt and ties it at the waist with one of her dad's vintage belts. She'll throw this over her cousin's old chicly torn black leggings, to which she has cleverly applied a row of her baby sister's diaper pins. The leggings, of course, are worn tucked into a pair of your next-door neighbor's Timberland castoffs. She's the kid who cooks up her own organic, environmentally sensitive makeup line, which she hustles successfully on the Web. She makes honor roll each term and manages to keep up with her friends, volunteer at an animal shelter, and skate in the local roller derby. Of course, she writes emo-folk-indie-rock songs with the adorable boy from down the street. He plays guitar. She sings. Yeah. Right. We've seen the movie.

REALITY BITES

Be honest. What "real" kid wants a wardrobe composed exclusively of hand-me-downs, thrift store finds, and swap-party originals? We'll wager not many. Don't get us wrong; we think the kid who has the taste and confidence to embrace vintage, funk, punk, Goth, boho, Salvation, Goodwill, or eBay rocks. It's just not likely to be your kid.

Remember, they are in the throes of identity building and are like heat-seeking missiles when it comes to targeting clothes that allow them to express the paradox of youth: independence and conformity. This is the time when "gently used" duds from an older sib, cousin, or friend can be deadly. You can try romancing hand-me-downs under the guise of vintage clothing. You can talk about being responsible citizens of the world and recycling. You can even try selling them on swapping, but the drive for something *they've* selected—fresh, new, and *just their own* (that may indeed be just like everyone else's)—has big curb appeal. (If you're the oldest and have never been at the end of the hand-me-down receiving line—trust us on this.)

ETSY LOVE

ETSY IS AN online marketplace that enables "people to earn a living making things, and to reconnect makers with buyers." We love the idea of buying directly from and supporting a worldwide collection of artisans and collectors. So crunchy and cool. Not to mention no crowds, no middleman, and best of all—for all us minding our budgets—no middleman markups.

If you're looking for kids' toys, clothes, or accessories, they have hundreds of thousands of items starting as low as $0.50 to as much as $700 (a custom-made princess dress).

FREEDOM'S (NOT) JUST ANOTHER WORD . . .

Still, we love thrift, vintage stores, swaps, Goodwill, and eBay for finding great and affordable bargains. Two notes of caution (we sound like such a mom): price and safety. Check pricing on things before you buy them. We've spied too many lies on eBay and in consignment where the articles of clothing are not really any bargain at all. Also, be wary of older products in general that might have been subject to recall, whether you're picking up toys and equipment or buying old sweatshirts or pants. Do not buy anything for a child with a string around the neck or waist that is not sewn in; these choking hazards by law can no longer be sold in stores, but will appear in resale shops. Don't forget, consignment and thrift go both ways: a great way to make back money you've spent and to give back to those in need.

Our favorite consignment story? A friend once stumbled upon an assortment of tunics and dresses that Janis Joplin would have rocked out in. With swirling paisleys, charming psychedelics, and fringe galore, these were Smithsonian-worthy garments. She got the lot for five bucks at Goodwill, washed them, and presented them to a teenager we knew, a thirteen-year-old hippie-in-training who roared with pleasure (a roar, we thought, not unlike Janis's). Generally reluctant to wear used clothes, this girl went crazy for the stuff, made the pieces her own, and received heaps of compliments, boosting her self-esteem. Then, when her hippie phase turned into a hipster phase (enter skinny jeans, V-neck tees, nerdy glasses), she sold those garments on eBay.

Let's just say she's no longer a snob about used clothes. These days she sells her own Goodwill finds on her Web site. *Cha-ching.*

THRED**UP**

CHECK OUT THREDUP (www.thredup.com), a simple way to exchange gently used clothing online. Imagine a box of gently used size 2T shirts or shorts filling out the spring wardrobe for five bucks a pop.

STITCH AND BITCH LIKE THEY USED TO

Everything old is new again, and there is nothing hipper or cooler these days than knowing how to DIY and be a creative crafter. Yup. Just like your grandma or great-aunt did, it's time to teach your kids to make their own clothes. Drag the sewing machine down from the attic, get a pair of knitting needles, dig up a crochet hook, and get to work. If you don't know, learn together. Imagine actually having something to show for your time—way more satisfying than wasting an evening cruising online shopping sites or watching *Project Runway* reruns. (Oh! Wait. Do this while you're watching *Project Runway* reruns.)

An entire generation of kiddie entrepreneurs, boys and girls, are crafting their own goodies and selling them—to neighbors, at local shops, at farmers' markets, online. . . .

CRAFTY

WE CAN KNIT a scarf, thread a needle and bobbin, do a little needlepoint, but we're not very talented. That doesn't stop us from cruising Ravelry, Etsy and Craftzine to chat with other knitters and to look at patterns and projects:

www.ravelry.com
www.etsy.com
http://craftzine.com/

Just remember, if they want to be the next kiddie mogul, keep it cool and low-key. If it's something they're truly passionate about doing, something that arises naturally, that's great. Our concern is when an interest of theirs becomes a passion of *yours*. Look, if James really wants to make a line of shampoos and body soaps just for boys, and Mary gets totally into her homemade leg warmers (now that she knows how to knit)—fantastic. Help them, facilitate the process. Don't push. When they grow weary of it, let it pass. They're kids, for goodness' sake.

ET TU, YOUTUBE?

JUST LIKE "THERE'S an app for that," there's a YouTube video for that, too. We're blown away by what you can learn on YouTube. Want to learn to knit and purl, crochet, sew a seam? Find a YouTube video.

WASH AND WEAR

Gender stereotyping is a nasty thing, to be sure, but eliminating home economics from school curricula was a little like tossing the baby out with the bathwater. While you might hope they'll grow up and have a staff, and they might believe they'll grow up and you'll still come and do their laundry, both boys and girls should learn the basics of ironing, sewing, and doing the laundry. (And cooking and cleaning and hammering and sawing and rewiring and changing the oil—or, at the very least, using the dipstick.)

These are the things you need to teach your kids to do. No excuses. If you don't know how or want to avoid another battle, there's a YouTube instructional video for this, too.

When it comes to dressing themselves and keeping their clothes in good repair, your kids should know how to:

- run the washing machine
- fold and put away clothes
- iron
- sew on a button
- hem a pair of pants; repair a ripped seam
- polish shoes

13

GIRLS AND BOYS AND SKIN AND CLOTHES AND BODY IMAGE
(and Your Wallet)

Got your attention?

There is no easy solution for the age-old parental worry about kids and sex. Remember chastity belts? Each generation confronts (or doesn't confront) their concerns in their own ways, just as each family passes on their values in their own way. Our rule is that you consciously face your own attitudes toward sex and gender roles, and work hard to pass on healthy attitudes to your blooming little cupcakes and stud muffins.

THE SEX TALK

To be frank, we're blushing and squirming a little in our seat, since we're not really sure if you're ready for this discussion. Truth be told, we're not really sure we're ready, but here we go.

This is a book about being a smart mom, and there are few

more permanent budget busters—time- and money-wise, that is—than a planned or unplanned pregnancy (yours or your kid-do's). So that's one thing. But *sex sells*. Not to go all Freudian or anything, but the marketplaces uses sex, and libidinal desire, to sell everything from books, to movies, to makeup, to clothes, to . . . well, you name it. This permeates our culture, and it's your responsibility to decode it for yourself and your kids.

Whether you're watching movie trailers for high school dramas, passing thong underwear for five-year-olds on store shelves, reading about the Biebs and his love nest on a Caribbean island in the tabloids, or watching Miley Cyrus doing a pole dance on television, sex and the promise of sex is everywhere. Even in the tween market—*especially* in the tween market. There is no getting away from it.

It's your job to help your sons and daughters grow up with a healthy attitude toward sex. It's your job to help them understand how the marketplace works, what messages they're receiving (and sending out), and to understand the line between safe and unsafe. It's your job to help them feel in control—even when the world, as it often will, seems out of control. They'll be healthier human beings for this, and you'll save loads of dough on tarty clothing.

GIRLS (AND BOYS, TOO), CLOTHES, AND SEXUAL OBJECTIFICATION

Later on we'll talk about healthy eating as a way of life that will help inoculate your child against obesity and other diseases. Conversations about sex and the media early on are a kind of inoculation against body-image problems, food disorders, anxiety, and overspending. These issues in girls (mostly) are in some measure brought on by the sexual objectification of women in our society at large, in the media, and by the continued use of frighteningly thin models.

So what can you do? Simple stuff. Talk about what you see. (Radical idea, right? Yet you'd be amazed how many forget to do this.) Analyze magazine advertisements and editorial content with your kids. Watch their favorite television shows with them. Be that annoying voice commenting that real people don't really do these things, as you all laugh.

Head to the store and look at magazines displayed on the racks: Add up how many feature barely clad women; keep a tally of the covers with headlines about how to have an orgasm; count the number that scream about ten ways to lose ten pounds in ten days. Watch *Jersey Shore*, *Keeping Up with the Kardashians*, or *The Bachelor* with them. Laugh, be amazed, and then talk about the way these shows are put together. They aren't "real" life, but casts thrown into a tightly controlled situation, plied with too much alcohol, and filmed. They're encouraged to act out in all kinds of risky ways; then it's edited for television to expose all the most sensational and outlandish behaviors.

Ask questions—what do your kids think of the tights-as-pants trend? How short is too short? Why do so many girls wear sweatpants that say "Juicy" on the rear? Keep a conversation going. Keep it informal, calm, curious. No smothering! Teach your kids about what a healthy BMI means. If they're not responsive to you, a good pediatrician or school counselor should help. And if you have concerns about their body image or eating habits, get involved pronto.

GOOD BOOKS ON SEX AND BODY IMAGE

Our Bodies, Ourselves: A New Edition for a New Era by the Boston Women's Health Book Collective

The Body Project by Joan Jacobs Brumberg

Packaging Girlhood: Rescuing Our Daughters from Marketers' Schemes by Sharon Lamb and Lyn Mikel Brown

IT'S NEVER TOO soon to tackle teaching them about the differences between girls and boys, so check out this book for the two-to-six-year-old set:

Who Has What? All About Girls' Bodies and Boys' Bodies by Robie H. Harris, illustrated by Nadine Bernard Westcott

When you keep these ideas in the air, it's more likely that when your kids are out shopping at the mall with their friends and stumble into Victoria's Secret or someplace even trashier (which they'll find), they'll think about the message they're sending with the "Hot Ass" underpants.

SIX-PACKS AND BOYS

DON'T FOR A minute think that gender stereotyping and unrealistic body and lifestyle imagining doesn't cut across the sexes. What eleven-year-old boy looks like a six-packed Abercrombie model? How about the ubiquitous beer commercials glorifying drinking and hooking up? Discuss with your sons the images of big cars, big cigars, drinking, and engaging in dangerous activities (*Jackass*, anyone?) in the drive to sell products by conveying unrealistic macho stereotyped behavior.

Want to learn more? Read *Packaging Boyhood: Saving Our Sons from Superheroes, Slackers, and Other Media Stereotypes* by Sharon Lamb, Lyn Mikel Brown, and Mark Tappan.

Trust us, you'll get nowhere pushing turtlenecks and baggy jeans on them. *Talk* to them, *listen* to them, but don't dictate their choices. Help your children be mindful consumers. They're going to live in the world, and they'll dress how they want to dress. Your job is to educate them so they make mindful choices. To support them. And—oh, yeah—to save money on crap.

Got that, mamas? Teach them that they can enjoy fashion and the media—without being their victims. Yes, there are lessons here for all of us.

PART 3

TEACHING THE PLEASURE OF FOOD:
A New Way, a New Day

INTRODUCTION

Unless you've been living under a rock, you know about the movement to eat healthy. You've watched *Jamie Oliver's Food Revolution* (so cute!), seen Mrs. O harvesting beets in the White House garden (even though hubby hates them), heard of Michael Pollan, and know that Monsanto, the chemical maker, somehow has something to do with desserts.

So you want to clean up the family diet. But you're confused about what you should be eating—and how to afford it. Maybe you wonder: Are whole grains really that much better? Is high-fructose corn syrup really that bad? Organic is the same as "all natural"—right?

Maybe you believe only rich people can afford to eat organic beef, microgreens, exotic grains.

Maybe, when faced with new food choices, you say, "My kids won't eat that stuff."

Maybe you're in a routine. You grab your coupons, run to the local market, throw the same mac 'n' cheese, roast, baby food, pasta, bottled tomato sauce, chicken fingers, and frozen pizza in your cart. Grab the juice, flavored yogurts, cookies, snacks, and chips. Fill up on the gallon of milk, butter, bread, eggs, and flee. It works, sort of.

Well, it's time for an educational update and a little attitude adjustment.

It's time to rethink the entire ritual around food: from planting to harvesting to shopping to preparing to eating. Food is a gift to family life. There is nothing optional about eating—so instead of making meals an in-and-out chore (there are way better quickies we can think of), make them a pleasure. A celebration. Make food a cornerstone of family life. Live better and have fun.

14

NEW BOUNDARIES, BETTER LIVING

YOUR JOB

Food is like all other aspects of parenting: Set clear boundaries and model appropriate behavior. Feel free to rant and rage about agribusiness and greed and the food supply; still the responsibility for feeding your kids a healthy diet is yours alone. (Sorry, we're not trying to guilt you or anything. Okay, well, maybe just a little.) It's up to you to provide good, balanced nutritional choices.

- It's your job to balance the food budget.
- It's your job to give your kids real and healthy food.
- It's your job to teach them to have reverence for the food they eat and respect for those who grow it.
- It's your job to create connected family mealtimes.
- It's your job to expose them to a broad range of food

choices—and this includes the real world of junk food. (Just as a kid totally denied television is likely to glue his eyes to any TV set he sees, a kid with no exposure to junk is likely to be lured by its taboo temptations. More on this later.)

- And, if you're really good at your job, your kids (and you) will have fun growing, gathering, and preparing the food you eat.

BANISH THE CRAP

Like everything in life, everything in moderation. We know it's not feasible to police every bite of food. So don't get nervous. While we wholeheartedly believe that you should eat whole-grain, heart-healthy, earth-friendly, good-for-you green stuff, we know that you can't possibly be "good" all the time. You have permission to occasionally skip 100 percent whole-wheat bread, to keep some junk on hand . . . but you *don't* have permission to keep your head in the sand on matters of nutrition.

So if you haven't already, it's time to get the premade processed junk *out* of your shopping baskets and your family diet. This crap is bad for you, bad for them, and expensive for a mom minding her wallet.

Your goal? To make lifelong healthy eaters so your kids can navigate and make smart food choices on their own.

DON'T BE A SLAVE TO OLD NEWS: FREE YOUR WALLET

Bet you can't tell us the latest government advisory on what you should be eating. It's hard to keep up. Remember the Food

Guide Pyramid posters that were plastered in the school cafeteria when you were a kid? Later this pyramid was replaced with the inscrutable MyPyramid, a guide so impenetrable it was sure to make any mummy proud. News flash: The pyramids have toppled.

Fortunately they've been replaced with a simpler and clearer set of dietary guidelines called MyPlate, and it's a big improvement! We love the first line in the new recommendations: "Enjoy your food, but eat less." The plate is divided into quarters, with veggies and fruits accounting for 50 percent of a healthy diet, grains accounting for 25 percent, and proteins the remaining 25 percent. On the table next to the plate is a setting for dairy.

A BIG FAT WAKE-UP CALL

	OBESITY RATE 1970s	OBESITY RATE 2007–08
KIDS 2–5	5%	10%
KIDS 6–11	4%	20%
KIDS 12–19	6%	18%
ADULTS	15%	34%

In 2008 thirty-two states had an adult obesity prevalence rate of more than 25 percent. This is in large contrast to the zero states weighing in with rates over 25 percent in the early 1990s.

(http://www.mypyramid.gov/guidelines/PolicyDoc.pdf)

We were pretty surprised to like it, since this is a document compiled by the U.S. Department of Health and Human Services *and* the United States Department of Agriculture. (The USDA is the federal agency responsible for promoting farm and agricultural products. . . . We don't have to tell you about all the special interests who must have had a voice in this, now, do we?) This may account for some of the lingering issues we have with the government's recommendations, like suggesting that only 50 percent of the grains come from whole-grain sources. Grains that are refined are just not as healthy as whole grains, so why split the difference? Also, the plate mixes apples and oranges, since three-quarters of it is composed of food groups (grains, fruits, veggies) and the other quarter nutrients (proteins). Why not directly address our need to reduce consumption of red meat? Why omit a discussion of healthy fats like olive oil and canola oil?

Okay, okay, we'll settle down. We're being such critics, and we *did* say it was a big improvement.

ILLUMINATING DIETS

OTHER RULERS HAVE built pyramids, too. We like the ones published by the Harvard School of Public Health Department of Nutrition and the Oldways Preservation Trust. And we're tickled that the Oldways pyramid shows people gathered, eating, and playing together. (Just like in the olden days!)

THE TAKEAWAY: GOOD-FOR-YOU FOOD + LESS OF IT = BUDGET-FRIENDLY

Eating healthy comes down to a few principles. Eat less and exercise more. Eat a diet loaded with fruits, vegetables, and whole grains. Eat a diet low in saturated fat and cholesterol. Eat more fish, less fatty meat. Dairy is no longer an integral part of the pyramid-turned-plate USDA recs but a side note, and should be fat-free or 1 percent. Closely monitor sugar and salt intake.

Cut out soda for the kids. Drink alcohol in moderation. (Remember your goal is just to be good—hey, no one's perfect.)

The good news is that this doesn't have to cost more; in fact, it should *save* you money. The foundations of a healthy diet—whole grains and fruits and veggies—are much more wallet-friendly than pricey meats. Plus take note of the first bit of advice: *Eat less.* Cut down your portion sizes. When you do buy meat, fish, or chicken, this will allow you to buy healthier hormone- and antibiotic-free products. (We are a nation consumed with big things, but bigger is not always better—you already know quality trumps size any day!)

Think about it: The more balanced your portion sizes, the less you will spend on your food budget. Plus, the more time spent exercising and playing, the less time spent shopping at the mall. (Trying clothes on and pulling your credit card out do not constitute healthy physical activities.)

A FUNNY DISH

CHECK OUT STEPHEN Colbert's riotous take on the new plate. Taking a sly shot at the amount of processed foods we eat, he says, "Americans don't use plates anymore. Our food comes from cases, bags, cans, tubes, and envelopes made of themselves."

(http://www.colbertnation.com/the-colbert-report-videos/ 388585/june-06-2011/obama-administration-replaces-food -pyramid)

THE READING LIST

READ SMART, UP-TO-DATE food writers like Marion Nestle, Mark Bittman, and Michael Pollan. The gist of their message would make our mom happy (see page 138), for they can all be boiled down to this: *Eat real food.* Try not to eat anything made with more than five ingredients. Try not to eat anything with something on the label you can't pronounce. Eat mostly plants. Eliminate (or reduce) processed foods. Eat less. Move more.

THE FOUNDATION: THE WHOLE GRAIN AND NOTHING BUT THE WHOLE GRAIN

But what is a whole grain, exactly?

A whole grain is made up of all the edible parts: the bran, the germ, and the endosperm. Simply stated, the bran is rich in fiber and B vitamins; the germ is also rich in B vitamins, along with healthy unsaturated fats and antioxidants; the endosperm is rich in complex carbohydrates and proteins.

LOOK FOR THE WHOLE-GRAIN LABEL

BUY PRODUCTS THAT are labeled "**100%** whole wheat." This is different from merely "whole wheat," which means the product contains only *some* whole wheat. Anything made from "enriched" flour is actually a refined grain with nutrients *added* back in. Want to know more? Find a list of whole grains and yummy recipes on our Web site: www.smartmamasmartmoney.com.

Not only are whole grains nutrient rich, they're also effective in the fight against overeating. Your munchkins will feel fuller longer, meaning no more shrieks of, "Maaaaa! I'm hungry!" every half hour.

Sounds good, now, doesn't it?

Best of all—contrary to what some believe—a diet rich in whole grains is not expensive. We repeat: *not expensive.*

EVEN THE BUGS KNOW BETTER

RICE AND FLOUR. Most of us know them as white, and grew up with them white. Why are they white? Because the brown parts (husks) contain all the nutrients, which bugs and bacteria (no dummies) love to eat while the food is in storage. In order to extend shelf life, manufacturers remove the germ and bran, leaving just the white stuff. So when you're eating anything that's white, you're not getting nearly as much nutritional value—and neither are your kids. Buy whole-grain whole-wheat flour and brown rice. Store in the fridge or freezer to preserve the good stuff.

15

ORGANIC, NATURAL, EAT
THIS AND LIVE FOREVER . . .
and Other Food Claims

Ladies, it's a jungle out there. A savvy mom must go shopping armed with a six-shooter and a magnifying glass. Just like you wouldn't send your tiny kids to a strange house to play without knowing the family, you need to know how the food you feed them was raised. Since we still don't have uniform, clear label regulations across all product categories, you need to be skeptical about product claims, ads, and the latest food fads.

Do you really believe eating Special K is going to make you lose weight? No. Eating *less* will help you lose weight. Think sugary cereals make your kids smarter? We have a bridge for sale. What about the juice bottle that shouts on the front, "Made without High-fructose Corn Syrup"? Check the fine print on the back and you'll most likely find it's loaded with sugar instead. (No, it's not better for you.) It's up to you to deconstruct what is good for you and your family.

THE BEEF WITH MEAT, CHICKEN, AND FISH

You're so damned tired at the end of a long day that when you rush into a grocery store your focus is to get in and out, to grab food for dinner at a price your budget allows. Who cares if the cow lived high on the hog or the fish swam in the open sea or the chicken was free to roam before the farmer clipped her wings?

You should care. Whether it's genetically modified crops and pesticides, unwanted antibiotics and hormones, or the inhumane industrial production of living animals releasing a host of contaminants into the environment, every thinking person on this planet should be paying close attention.

Even if you're heartless and don't give a rat's a** about the animals for the animals' sake, you'd better care for the health of your kids. The sh*t they feed these animals is not good for your little ones.

Animals and fish are not machine parts. Yet we have industrialized the way we raise them in concentrated animal feeding operations (CAFOs) and aquaculture farms. They're crowded together in concrete pens, cages, and coops, unnaturally pumped up on growth hormones, and routinely administered prophylactic antibiotics in response to the ailments brought on by overcrowding, unnatural diets, and inhumane "living" conditions.

Not all fish, meat, or chicken is raised this way, so it's up to you to find the good stuff for your family. Remember, you're feeding this to your kiddos. . . . What's the point of saving money on products that could possibly compromise their health? Besides, since you're paring down this portion of their diet as you increase grains, fruits, and veggies, you can afford to step it up.

YOUR MAMA WAS WRONG: THERE AREN'T PLENTY MORE FISH IN THE SEA

While aquaculture is the long-term solution for depleted fishing stocks, it has opened up a whole new can of worms. From fish fed pellets (often composed of nasty components), stewing in unsanitary water, and routinely given antibiotics, to the possibility of genetically altered fish escaping pens and breeding with ocean fish, aquaculture has changed the way we look at fish when we're in the market.

Think about this: Farm-raised salmon is gray in color from eating processed pellets of food. That lovely bright pink glistening shade you see in fish in the case is selected from a color chart—just like picking deep salmon for the walls in the dining room—and achieved through a color additive. Yuck. In the same vein, much of the shrimp you buy in stores frozen (or previously frozen) comes from overseas shrimp farms. Hello! We can complain, and we will, about the inability of our government to successfully regulate and oversee farms and food makers in this country. Who can possibly police foreign suppliers?

Still, there are some wonderful and ethical aquatic farmers out there. How do you know the good from the bad? It's not easy. A smart mom needs to be comfortable that the store she is shopping at is sourcing fish from purveyors who engage in good farming practices.

Ask.

EDUCATE YOURSELF:
You Are What You Eat

- Enter the Meatrix. Take this animated tour around an industrial farm. It's eye-opening and disturbing—and it's only a cartoon (www.themeatrix.com)!
- If you haven't seen them yet, rent *Food, Inc.* and *Fast Food Nation.*
- Every fish-feeding mom should stay up-to-date with the recommendations from the folks at the Monterey Bay Aquarium's Seafood Watch (www.montereybayaquarium.org/cr/seafood watch.aspx). Stay on top of which fish are high in methylmercury and the guide to safe serving sizes; look for their recommendation on safe-to-eat aquaculture species and their countries of origin; be aware of which fish are on watch lists because of overfishing. Their data is updated regularly and lets you select your region for recommendations that balance sustainability and health concerns. (And bring your family to this aquarium if you're in the area . . . more educational bang for your buck than any other we've seen.) There's also an app for that: Download their app on your mobile to find out if that fish in the market is red-, yellow-, or green-lighted for dinner tonight.

ORGANIC, ALL-NATURAL, AND OTHER CLAIMS

"Organic" and "natural" are not the same.

USDA regulations defining "organic" are specific when it comes to meat, poultry, fresh produce, and dairy, less black-and-white when it comes to packaged goods, and nonexistent when it comes to fish. "Natural" on a food label is purely artificial. It means nothing. Outside of a narrow and useless definition in the cooked-meat-and-poultry arena, anyone can call anything natural.

According to the regulations, "Organic food is produced without using most conventional pesticides. Fertilizers have no synthetic ingredients or sewage sludge. No genetic or bioengineering of seeds or iodizing radiation is permitted. All food must be certified by the government to get a certificate." This also means that the food supply of all animals must also be certified organic, and there is no routine use of prophylactic antibiotics and no synthetic growth hormones. When it comes to meat, fruit, poultry, milk, and eggs, products are either 100 percent organic or not. Period.

Regarding organic on the labels of packaged goods, it's a little more confusing. Since many ingredients go into making a cracker, for example, the rules differ. You can find 100 percent organic, 95 percent organic, or "made with organic ingredients" (which can mean anything).

THE WHOLE STORY

WANT TO KNOW more? One of the clearest and simplest-to-understand FAQ sheets on organic, natural, and transitional products has been done by Whole Foods Market (http://www.wholefoodsmarket.com/values/organic-faq.php#5).

When it comes to everything else in the food business, manufacturers are free to call their foods "all-natural" no matter what they contain, and studies have shown that some consumers believe this is better for them than organic. Don't fall for this.

Don't pay more for these products. Don't be duped into thinking you're feeding the kids something better.

FOOD LABELS: THE SMART STATUS SYMBOL

Do not trust manufacturer's claims . . . you know, like you'll cheat death by drinking their juice, lose weight by eating their ice cream, kill germs by sucking their mints. As of this writing, a panel of experts is making recommendations to simplify and put on the front of all packaged products the key things every consumer must know about the ingredients. In the meantime it's up to you to know how to read the ingredient label on the *back* of every package.

LOST IN TRANSLATION

Understanding a food label can be like translating a foreign language. Learn at How to Read a Label: http://www.fda.gov/food/labelingnutrition/consumerinformation/ucm078889.htm.

Two Key Concepts

- Know that the first-named ingredient on a list constitutes the biggest part of the product. So if you're buying apple juice and the first ingredient on the label is high-fructose corn syrup, uh, you're not buying apple juice.

- Simplify. Banish confusion before it begins. Apply the five-ingredient-or-fewer rule to most products. If you've never heard of or can't pronounce the ingredients, take a pass.

ORGANIC DOESN'T MEAN CLEAN

ORGANIC FOOD IS still grown in fields. Still handled by lots of hands. And grown "without using *most* conventional pesticides." Moral of the story? Organic still needs to be washed—thoroughly.

PRODUCE TO INVEST IN

When it comes to fruits and veggies, we keep in mind the Environmental Working Group's 2011 shopping list of the "dirty dozen" (most likely to be contaminated with pesticides) and the "clean fifteen" (lowest in pesticides). This way, our hard-earned bucks go to those with most risk.

DIRTY DOZEN	CLEAN FIFTEEN
Apples	Onions
Celery	Corn
Strawberries	Pineapples
Peaches	Avocado
Spinach	Asparagus
Nectarines	Sweet Peas
Grapes	Mangoes
Sweet Bell Peppers	Eggplant
Potatoes	Cantaloupe
Blueberries	Kiwi

Lettuce	Cabbage
Kale/ Collard Greens	Watermelon
	Sweet Potatoes
	Grapefruit
	Mushrooms

NO HORMONES IN THE MILK, MOTHER

Milk products are one place a mama should be smart and buy organic if at all possible. Research shows that the nasty hormones that are routinely given to cows to stimulate growth pass through into their milk. If organic isn't an option, make sure the labels of all your milk products say, "No rBGH." This means cows haven't been given recombinant bovine growth hormone. This stuff's bad for you and your kids. Period.

THE BOTTOM LINE

We don't want to eat fish that's been fed chicken pellets; we don't want meat jacked-up on hormones; we don't want chicken pumped full of antibiotics; we don't want pesticide-laden fruits and veggies. So our first choice is to buy local and know how our food is grown. In the supermarket, we use organic as a shorthand—to tell us that there are fewer nasties in the mix. When the organic offering is just too pricey, select fish, chicken, and meats that are antibiotic- and hormone-free. For fruits and veggies bear in mind the EWG dirty dozen.

CALL FOR HELP

NOT SURE ABOUT how to discover the provenance of your food? Ask. Check with the person selling the fish or the meat or the milk or the cheese or the produce in your local store. Reputable suppliers and stores are onto this and more than happy to talk with you about their policies. Actually, we've had some so eager to wax poetic on the wax-free fruit we thought we'd never escape.

LAND CATCHES YOU CAN AFFORD

Hormone-, antibiotic-, and pesticide-free products can be expensive. Watch for specials. Remember, supermarkets break down their goods by departments, and the seafood guys need to come up with weekly deals just like their sisters running the grocery aisles, meat counters, produce stands, and dairy cases. When you find a bargain, snag it. Stew it up or seal it away and store in the freezer for a later date.

Enough processing?

Now, how to find the good stuff.

16

GETTING THE GOODS:
Where Empowered Moms
Go for Sustenance

In our fantasy food world, there'd be one bustling street with a butcher, a baker, a cheese store, a fishmonger, a local fruit-and-veggie purveyor, and a woman-owned-and-operated sex toy boutique—uh, sorry. Went a little overboard there. Let's stick to food.

Since you don't live in the nineteenth century, you'll be hunting and gathering at both big-box stores and local providers. While the boxsters aren't perfect, when money feels like a nonrenewable resource, something's gotta give, and Costco, BJ's, and Sam's offer big value. Find a local source for bulk grains (organic if you're lucky enough to find a good place). As much as you can, fill in your daily fresh-food needs at your local farmers' market or food co-op. We know this isn't always possible, so shop smart at Whole Foods, Wegmans, even Walmart. (Yup, we said it! This is not without controversy, but we're realists, and when the largest company in the world jumps into the game it's a giant step in the right direction. They've signed up for improving sourcing and supporting the sustainable/organic movement.)

Finally, make it your business to participate in a CSA (community-supported agriculture) arrangement and plan to plant your own garden.

THE SHOPPING STRATEGY

Smart moms start with a list of category needs and stay flexible—this is better for your budget and will yield better-quality food. Seasonal fruits and vegetables as they come to harvest offer the best value; markets cut deals with suppliers. You may find great prices on Brussels sprouts and pears one week, on string beans and strawberries the next. If you're planning on a big Sunday cooking session and have recipes in mind, don't be rigid. If thighs are on sale, sub them in for breasts. Or better yet, when you find on sale the basic cuts your family prefers, stock up. This is one of the reasons we think of recipes as guidelines and are never slaves to ingredients (okay, the real reason is we're snarly and don't follow rules very well).

FILL UP THE LARDER HERE

Approach food shopping in that schizoid state every mother knows all too well: Be both flexible and controlling.

Before we begin, we offer these disclaimers: We do not own stock in any of the following companies (although we wish we had bought some years ago). We do think farmers are hot, but are not married to one or dating one.

SMALL POTATOES

Farmers' Markets and Farm Stands

"Buy local" is on everyone's lips. Why buy apples from New Zealand if you live near an orchard in Seattle? Yes, you long to travel the world, but please don't live vicariously through your fruit. We love nothing more than yummy fresh, local produce. There is nothing more nutritious. Eat your way through the progression of the local farmers' crops: arugula, lettuces, strawberries, rhubarb, asparagus, beans, beets, blueberries, broccoli, cabbage, carrots. For the best deals, buy as the harvest peaks, when there's local abundance.

Locally grown food helps reduce the carbon footprint—just think about the energy used to transport the Chilean grape to Bangor. You'll get to know how what you're eating is grown. You may get to say hello to the person who grew it. We think it's kind of like knowing the family of your child's prospective mate (the older our kids get, the more we understand arranged marriages).

KNOW THY BACKYARD

WE LOVE LOCAL Harvest, a go-to resource that connects you to farmers' markets, co-ops, and CSAs near you. Check out their fantastic Web site devoted to sustainable food (www.localharvest.org). You may be surprised by the options in your own neck of the woods.

Get Your Crunch On: Join a Food Co-op

What's old is new again. Those hippies were onto something when it came to community organizing and sharing as a way of life. While we're not advocating burning your bra and scouring secondhand stores in search of overalls (well, maybe we are—see page 82), we think working one afternoon or evening a week at a co-op *with your kids* is a great way to buy healthy (often organic) foods for less. It's also a terrific way to be part of a community, and to teach a thing or two about commerce to your little ones.

BUY THE WHOLE ENCHILADA

WELL, NOT REALLY. More like the whole pig, lamb, or cow. If you have a really *big* freezer, consider buying the entire animal (or half an animal) and sharing it with friends. The local farm near us sells quarters or halves of ethically raised critters.

Advanced Moms Get CSAs

Community-supported agriculture is an opportunity to buy a share in a farmer's harvest from a local grower. The idea is that you share the risk with Ms. Greenjeans, and your seasonal share entitles you to a portion of whatever your local farmer yields. Each CSA is independent, and, as of this writing, we know of several thousand around the country. Do research before you make an agreement. While it's not common, we've heard of people who've been disappointed in the management of the farm or the way the shares were allocated. And if the farmers' crops fail, so, too, might your investment.

This is not for the faint of heart; one month you may end up with five pounds of kale, an entire year's worth of onions, and no tomatoes (the ones you were salivating over all summer). You'll need to be flexible about what you cook, and willing to experiment with new recipes. Our recommendation is to give it a try with a friend or two. The experience of going to the farmer with your kids (although many farmers bring their harvest to a central drop-off spot), and of having ownership in the food chain, is priceless.

In our area there is even a CSA delivering fresh fish weekly—Cape Ann Fresh Catch—supported by the Gloucester Fishermen's Wives Association. Pretty cool!

Specialty Markets

Every city and town has small markets that stock ethnic, regional, or specialty products. Our city has a market that specializes in hard-to-find spices from around the world. We love taking the kids to chat with the owner, sampling new tastes and flavors. (It doesn't hurt they have an ice-cream shop next door that makes fantastic concoctions.) Asian markets are like entering a new country—the assortments are often bewildering, always exciting. Best of all, the prices are so low we can't figure out how they stay in business. We love the Portuguese market that sells homemade and backyard smoked linguiça and chorizo, as well as the freshest and biggest assortment of local fish in the area—their overhead is low and the pricing follows.

Take your kids and go exploring. It's cheaper than getting on a plane to Morocco or a boat to the Azores.

SAVINGS COME IN ALL FORMS: The Mighty Leftover, and Eat the *Whole* Thing

BUY WHOLE CHICKENS, whole fish, roasts with bones. Cut them up yourself—or if you're squeamish, have the butcher or fishmonger do it for you—and reserve the bones in a freezer bag. Once you have a critical mass, haul them out and use them as a base for soups. Into the soup add leftovers from a few days of cooking: faro, green beans, roasted garlic . . . you'd be surprised what you can create. Buy beets with greens. Roast the beets. Steam the greens. Recipe calls for yolks? Save the whites and make meringues. You get the idea.

Of course, you're already saving by packing lunches made from leftovers. Right?

BIG POTATOES

Whole Foods

Whole Foods gets a bad rap for being overly expensive. Some items are pricey, to be sure, but you *can* get in and out with good healthy offerings for a reasonable sum—if you're smart about it. What we like is not worrying about things like artificial food dyes and additives—forbidden. The fish is carefully bought and the assortment of organic and additive-free meats is unrivaled (outside of organic specialty stores). We give them kudos for their wide grain, cheese, pasta, coffee, and tea assortments. But if you're buying frozen food, check the package for the country of origin. We've been disappointed to find "organic" frozen veggies grown in China sold under the Whole Foods 365 brand. We have no confidence in food sourced from places where oversight is difficult.

First stop is the fruit and vegetable aisles. While we try to keep the carbon footprint of our purchases small, it's not always possible in the dead of winter, when local farms are buried under three feet of ice-capped snow. Buy seasonal: Bags of mangoes on sale in March. Citrus in December. Apples in September.

Greens are plentiful and something's always on sale. Our latest obsession has been eating deep-green leafy greens like kale, collard, and dandelion. Incredibly healthy, simple to make, and not expensive.

Skate over to the fishmonger and ask her what just came in. While we prefer fresh-caught ocean fish, Whole Foods has reasonably stringent standards for farm-raised. Grab a pound of fish on sale, marinate it in garlic and ginger, throw it on the grill with some sweet potatoes, and steam up a serving of dandelion greens. Cross over to the poultry case and find value-priced family-size packs of chicken thighs or turkey legs. Coat them with a spice rub, throw them in the oven, and serve with quinoa and broccoli for a simple midweek dinner.

Clean up in the bulk aisles. All organic and all under three bucks a pound: panko flakes, $2.99/pound; organic brown rice, $1.39/pound; whole-wheat couscous, $2.79/pound; whole-grain Kamut® wheat, $1.99/pound; barley, $1.69/pound; the entire assortment of bulk dried beans, all under $1.99/pound. Who said eating healthy and eating organic is expensive?

YOGURT SLUTS

GREEK-STYLE NONFAT PLAIN yogurt is versatile and a good source of calcium and protein. Don't buy presweetened, prefruited yogurt. Make it yourself. Fresher. Healthier.

We're yogurt sluts and go with whoever is offering us a good deal, be it name brand or store: Chobani, Fage, Trader Joe's brand. (The warehouse clubs have the very best price on Chobani we've found.)

It's great for breakfast or a snack with fresh fruit and a drizzle of honey. We'll make homemade preserves and top the yogurt with them, or have it as a sundae substitute with walnuts, bananas, and honey. It makes a great base for a healthy dip. And on a hot summer night with fresh-cut veggies and tomatoes, it makes a refreshing dinner.

Costco . . .

Loving to shop in an airplane hangar must say something about us. So jet-set. Temptation lurks around every corner. Move fast and stay focused on your target purchases. You don't need a new vacuum or new wide-screen television, no matter how cheap they are. Keep moving.

Head straight to the food area. Be wary. You'll encounter the food pushers with the hook: yummy samples made from processed products filled with a laundry list of fake ingredients. You know, the double-fried burrito served with spicy guac dipping sauce. Those tiny bites in the frilly white paper cups are really good after a long day. It doesn't help that you and the kids are starving and they're stomping their feet and guilting you with, "C'mon, Mom, I like it; you never buy anything we like to eat."

Okay. You can break down sometimes; hey, we all do. But make it occasional food (think *Star Trek*—see below), not family fare.

. . . OR SAM'S, OR BJ'S

WHILE WE'RE BIG Costco shoppers, feel free to sub in your box-ster of choice. Just be careful; these big guys can get a girl into trouble. Bring a list and stick to it!

Once you've finished your free lunch and been shamed into throwing the bag of frozen burritos into your cart, it's time to get down to real business. Just remember two things: No more processed food (that bag of burritos is it), and bulk buys are good buys only when you can actually use the whole enchilada before it goes bad. Control yourself. Or shop with a friend and agree to split the three-pound bargain bag of garlic for $5.69, the ten-pound bag of potatoes for $6.99, or the huge hands of bananas for $.43. Pick up bags of lettuce, bunches of asparagus, packs of peppers for half the price you'll find elsewhere.

Costco's our destination for Parmigiano Reggiano, President feta, and Cabot extra-sharp cheddar. Their fish and meat areas are low-priced and high-quality. (Though we're not too sure of the meat's and fish's lineage, and, with few organic options, we resist making this our go-to meat destination. But we'd be lying to say we never bite.) Organic poultry offerings clock in under Whole Foods pricing—but just barely.

Throw in an eight-pack of Barilla whole-wheat pasta. Grab the giant Heinz ketchup, the two-pack of Grey Poupon mustard, and the six-pack of Kirkland organic chicken stock. Say no to the industrial-size Hellmann's mayo. Say yes to the Kirkland extra-virgin olive oil. (We have yet to find a Kirkland-brand product we don't like.)

GET YOUR GRIND ON

GRIND YOUR OWN meats. It's cheap. It's better for you. It's better-tasting. When you buy your own cuts, you get to select the best-quality pieces and have control over the freshness of the product. We always buy a fresh cut from the butcher, bring it home, and grind it ourselves. The end product is more flavorful and lighter than store-bought preground. Too much work, you say? Not really. It's remarkably easy. We use our grandmother's old hand grinder. Simple to set up. Easy to clean. When you grind it yourself you have control over the quality of what your family eats and control over the sanitary conditions that go into the grind. Think about this: Most ground meat and premade patties sold in stores are made from the trimmings and ends of cuts from multiple animals. Yuck. Grind it yourself and avoid having to worry every time there is a recall of premade patties or bulk ground meat.

Give it a crank.

Whiz down the aisles; look askance at the empty-nutrition/high-calorie Starbucks Frappuccinos, the juice drinks that aren't really juice, and the bad-for-you soda assortments. Fill up on sparkling water and club soda to make healthy, homemade flavored fizzy drinks. Skip the large packaged coffee bags, unless you run a diner. The bags are too big and likely to turn stale before you use them up—not to mention the coffee is mediocre.

While we're insisting you drop all that soda crap from your diet, we're not expecting you to give up all your spirited libations. Costco is the place we pick up wine, vodka, and whiskey.

The prices are outstanding, and their product offering is top-rate. Our advice is to bring home a few different sample bottles before you spring for a case. The mainstay of our vodka assortment is the Kirkland brand (rumor has it it's made by Grey Goose, and it's half the price), but the bottle is *jumbo*, and we must admit we're a little embarrassed to be seen toting it around.

And since buying toilet paper, diapers, toothpaste, dog food, and laundry detergent is as satisfying as buying oil for the car, make this the place for the one-stop, in-and-out bulk-up.

COSTCO OR AMAZON DIRECT?

WE READ AN interesting article a while back in which a *New York Times* reporter did a test of which was cheaper for all his bulk purchases—Costco or Amazon's Subscribe & Save. Costco won. (http://www.nytimes.com/2011/03/05/your-money/05money.html/)

Trader Joe's

We love Joe, but he's just not a reliable stop for daily living. The produce and meats are variable. We never know what will be in stock, and, more to the point, we never know if it will be good-looking. We can find great pricing on bananas ($.19) but may not like the look of the green beans and broccoli.

But what Joe does well he excels at. We won't go anywhere else for dried fruits like raisins and apricots; walnuts, almonds, and hazelnuts; organic Valencia peanut butter (the best) and other nut butters.

Folks swear by TJ's frozen fish, like halibut and wild Alaskan salmon. Take a pass on the scallops—frozen scallops tend to be too watery—and don't forget what we told you about farm-raised fish. (Bring your smartphone and check in with Monterey Bay Aquarium's Seafood Watch.)

Stash away bags of frozen veggies for those days fresh supplies are low. You'll find good deals at TJ's on organic frozen peas, broccoli, green beans.

We always leave with fresh flowers in hand—the biggest floral bargains in our area are right at TJ's front door. Nothing—well, almost nothing—puts a smile on our face like a bright bunch of red anemones or yellow tulips.

A LIST FOR SMART SHOPPING

- Look for sale items on end caps—they've been purchased at an advantageous price from the supplier; the savings are then passed on to you.

- Avoid large feature presentations not on sale, since they are probably precursors to sale events, and the retailer is trying to get as much full-priced business before the sale event as possible (like the stores with cashmere sweaters).

- Use the unit pricing as a guide to find the best buy. Just make sure the basis for the unit pricing is comparing apples to apples. For example, you can buy tea either loose or in bags. The loose tea will be measured by ounce, the bagged tea by quantity.

- The house brand's lowest-priced products are often the cheapest available in a category.

- Pay attention to expiration dates. Unless you are going to be using it right away, a bargain with a short shelf life is no bargain.

- Most retailers want to get you in the door with highly recognizable items, such as lettuce, ketchup, or cans of tomatoes, either on sale or at an everyday low price— check circulars.

- During holiday or seasonal events, find great deals on seasonal items like hams and chocolate bunnies at Easter. The trade-off is that you're unlikely to find great prices on the higher-quality end of the spectrum, because this is where a market makes its money. So in November you can probably get a Butterball turkey at a great price (ah, not our fave), but finding a bargain on a whole, fresh, locally raised organic turkey may be difficult.

- Do *not* buy health and beauty aids at the grocery store; they are sold as a convenience to the shopper and you will likely pay full margin unless they are on sale.

COUPONS: A Rant

WE HATE COUPONS.

They add burden and guilt to our already overburdened and overguilty lives. Why don't the manufacturers and retailers just throw that money back into reducing the everyday price of their products? Besides, think about it; it would be a mercy killing of that bizarre *Extreme Couponing* show on TLC.

People end up with products they would never, ever buy—maybe don't even want—just because there's a coupon attached. Plus, so much of the processed crap is being promoted through coupons. Ugh!

What really set us off was reading about the apps for smart-phones that allow you to scan at the register everything that's in your basket that has a "deal" attached to it. Huh? What is the point? Why not just have the registers scan for any promotional discount attached to a product? Boom, it's over. Put a discreet sign in the aisle: MAMA MAY'S MIGHTY MAYO 20 PERCENT OFF NOW THROUGH SUNDAY—DISCOUNT TAKEN AT THE REGISTER. If you want it, grab it.

How about a fair exchange? Fair pricing. Fair profit.

Buy products you like, products you use, products you need. Don't buy something just because the manufacturer is hustling you with a coupon, unless you'd use it anyway.

(We feel so much better.)

17

SNICKERING CITY DWELLERS & LAPSED DIY'ERS:
Time to Get Your 4-H On!

So much for hunting and gathering; it's time to progress to the agrarian era and harness the power of your own two hands—and your kids' hands. It's time to start digging. Save money. Be healthy. Have fun.

IT'S NO SECRET—PLANT A VICTORY GARDEN

What's a victory garden? We'd heard the expression; we even own Marian Morash's *The Victory Garden Cookbook*, but we'd never given it much thought, except as an expression of triumph of woman over nature. After all, anyone who's ever planted, nurtured, and harvested a successful vegetable garden knows it's a war: You versus weather. You versus rabbits. You versus cutworms. You versus poaching neighbors. (You know the ones: "Oops! We thought you were gone for the summer! We didn't want the blueberries to go to the birds!" Of course, you never go anywhere and were just out picking up the dry cleaning.)

The term "victory garden" comes from the Second World War, when fresh produce was in short supply. Patriotic, scurvy-fearing citizens dug up their yards and planted beans, corn, cucumbers—whatever their climate zone would bear. At harvest-time they canned and preserved their bounty.

If you have any room at all (a yard, a deck, a rooftop, a windowsill), this is an ideal project for you and your family. Think of this as a fight for victory over your pocketbook, Monsanto, and the mall. Successful gardens can provide a cycle of in-season fresh vegetables and fruits, and out-of-season frozen and canned stores. Besides, better to have a child who's a garden bunny than a mall rat. Just like having a pet teaches responsibility, nurturing, and the life cycle, so does growing a garden. From seed to table, a child will value the food he grows, will feel ownership, will be less likely to waste and complain. Think of this as yet another opportunity to teach them about hard work, success, failure, and control—or, as the case may be, lack of control. (We'll pretend for a moment that you've mastered your own control issues.) Just like no mom ever thinks her baby is ugly, a cabbage grown in your *own garden* is more likely to be admired and cuddled and kissed. Uh, we mean eaten.

GREEN-A-LOT

URBAN GARDENS ARE springing up everywhere—stories of people growing for their own needs, growing to help feed neighbors, growing to teach inner-city kids about the food cycle. It's exciting! Grow with them: http://www.cityfarmer.info/category/united-states/.

RETURN TO EDEN: PLANT FRUIT TREES

One of our fondest childhood recollections is accompanying our parents to a nursery, selecting plum, pear, and peach trees, and then coming home to plant them in a yard that seemed huge (but in retrospect was no larger than a postage stamp). The grown-ups' excitement was infectious the first year those trees bore fruit. Our memory of late summer is of ripening fruit, of the sweet smell in the yard, of rushing out to pick plums, comparing the sweetness of the peaches and the Italian plum varieties, of happily bagging them and sharing them at school with friends. To this day when we see small sweet Italian plums in the store we can't help but fill a bag to overflowing.

Take your toddler and plant some trees. Watch them grow together.

PRESERVE THE OLD WAYS

WHAT TO DO with nature's bounty? Preserve it, of course. Make jams, jellies, pickled pickles, beets, okra. (For recipes, see our Web site: www.smartmamasmartmoney.com.)

GONE FISHING

Depending on where you live, your outdoor spirit, and how polluted the waterways are, this is another activity for you and your kids to do together. We live on the coast, and while fishing stocks are no longer as bountiful as once upon a time, there's always something to be caught or dug up. Warning: Don't get carried away with excess "gear"; expensive implements are truly not necessary. Resist the urge to look the part! Borrow or buy used rods, drop-fishing lines, digging tools. Send Junior out to get the worms. We love to dig clams and harvest scallops. No fancy tools required. Seasonal conditions (and an inexpensive license) are all that are required. We'll spend a morning gathering, an afternoon cleaning and shucking, and then fresh-freeze our catch for the winter.

READ ALL ABOUT IT

YOU'RE TEACHING YOUR kids to revere nature. Now reinforce your message with good books. Talk to your local librarian about books to accompany whatever activity you're involved in. Our faves? For little ones, no one beats Robert McCloskey—check out *One Morning in Maine* and *Blueberries for Sal*. As they get older, stick a copy of *The Secret Garden* in their hands—all about the power of nature and friendship to revitalize the soul. Teenagers must read *Adventures of Huckleberry Finn* for (among other remarkable lessons) bringing home the power and vitality of the Mississippi River. Once your little ones have grown big literary minds, pass them Laura Esquivel's *Like Water for Chocolate*, a magical novel about a young woman who can express herself only by cooking—and who finds love in the most unexpected (and delicious) of circumstances.

RAISE CHICKENS! NO YOLK.

Really, no joke. Advanced moms raise more than kids. While we personally don't have chickens squawking in our yard, we have friends who do. This is for the advanced, go-to-the-head-of-the-class earth mom. Start with a few chicks (and live where there is no street for them to cross). Unlike dogs and indoor pets, you won't have to worry about walking them. They'll actually give you something in return: eggs. Your own fresh, free-range, environmentally friendly little yolkers.

TAKE A PEEK

THINKING OF RAISING your own? Wondering what a backyard flock would be like? Just wondering in general what it would be like to raise things in your backyard? We love this blog: www .hencam.com/henblog/.

Now you've got the goods; it's time to bring them home.

18

SLOW DOWN PROGRESS:
Twenty-first-century Eating

Every book, parenting expert, and Oprah special tells you how important it is to eat meals together, that if you don't your child is sure to be incarcerated at a young age, run off and join a cult, abuse drugs. What they don't talk about are the logistical difficulties of getting everyone in one room at the same time, the challenge of actually cooking and getting a meal on the table, the struggles around cleanup time, and the often silent or screaming group dramas that play out at the table.

The advice experts certainly aren't inside your vibrating body, exhausted from your day at work. They're not with you during your day at home with the kids, your day as a chauffeur running elderly relatives to the doctor, your day racing to be on time for day-care pickup, your day taking kids to and from lessons and sports, your day fighting with the insurance company over car/health/property-damage claims, your day hunting for the lost dog, no-show cable repair guy, missing mittens. We feel your pain.

Finally you get everyone at the table, and your tot has a meltdown, and Susie complains she can't stand pasta with red sauce when you know for a fact that's all she would eat for the past two months, even though now she indignantly informs you she has never—*never!*—liked pasta with red sauce. More proof positive that you care only about "the baby" and you fail to pay attention to her needs. Johnny is having romantic difficulties with his girlfriend, can't bear to be separated from his cell phone, and, since he is a boy (and a teen), is stubbornly sullen and silent. Your partner (if they're in the picture) is late again, but promised they'd be on time this time, and will be disappointed when you start without them. You really want to be a "good" family-meal mom, but containing the kids who haven't eaten for at least an hour is more than you can bear. Oh, not to mention that you're *starving*.

Yes, we know varying schedules or varying ages make it really hard! But your job is to be organized enough to be able to put a healthy, simple meal on the table and have the fortitude to withstand the whining and complaining. So when you're all home at mealtime, seize the chance to convene as a family with no TV watching, no texting while scarfing, no McDonald's, no leaning over the sink to wolf down that Costco microwaved burrito.

Now you're asking: *How, exactly, do I manage this?*

We hear your foot tapping.

Here's how.

IN THE FOOD BUSINESS, EVERYONE HAS A JOB

It's your little tot's job to play, your middle schooler's job to take out the trash, your job to bring home the bacon. Everyone in a family has work to do. Since you're in charge of this army (is the power getting to your head yet?), it's your responsibility to make a meal plan for your troops to execute.

This will require a little planning and family discussion, which are good for your kids, teaching them real skills and a sense of responsibility. And which are good for you, too, since you'll get real help, making it possible to sit down together for family mealtime.

Assemble the draftees and compile a list of food-related chores. Our recommendation is that you assign chores on a rotating schedule. One week dishwasher unloading, one week dishwashing, one week taking out the garbage and composting. If you've planted a victory garden, assign weeding, watering, and harvesting duties.

Cooking together is fun and creative. Make it part of your Sunday routine. Gather your clan and cook for the week ahead. It will save you money; it will save you time; and, believe us, when your kids are the authors of a meal, you're likely to eliminate the "I don't like this" whine (which, as you know, sends you to the real wine). Wash and prepare all those fresh veggies, stew up a pot of chili, make a lasagna, bake a cake, concoct granola and trail mix. Crank up the music, cook to a favorite cooking show, watch the football game. Just make it fun.

Let your kids learn how to barter. If one particularly hates unloading and doesn't mind washing, or if one has a particularly heavy homework schedule or a game after school, let them negotiate a trade.

Of course, since you're a mom, you'll end up letting them off the hook more often than not, but you're teaching them valuable lessons: planning, negotiating, thinking about more than just themselves.

SLICE AND DICE

CUT UP SEVERAL kinds of veggies on Sunday for the week ahead: cauliflower, broccoli, carrots, celery—whatever is seasonal and abundant. Put in snack bags, use as a side dish at dinner. Send them to school with hummus or peanut butter as a dip. Use one night as a mix for a stir-fry.

SAY GOOD-BYE TO THE CLEAN PLATE CLUB

Whether it's a baby that looks like Jabba the Hutt or an eight-year-old with pants that won't stay up, at some point (and often over the very same kid), every parent frets that his or her kid is too small, too big, too whatever. It's totally normal. Hey, if you aren't worrying, what kind of mom are you?

Rather than turning each meal into a battleground, it's smarter to teach your kids to eat until they're not hungry rather than eat to being full. There is *no need* for them to be polishing their dish clean—that's why you have a dishwasher. Yes, you want to teach your kid to value food, to take reasonable portions, to eschew waste. But you also want them to learn how to read and trust their bodies. Remember, when it comes to offering food, a meal is just like every other aspect of being a good parent: You need to offer them good choices and respect what they like and don't like.

Easy for us to say. You have the kid who eats only white things: white bread, marshmallow fluff, chicken breast, white fish, mayonnaise, cauliflower (at least it's a vegetable), butter, mac 'n' cheese. We're sorry. Have you considered bleach? Only kidding! Vow to keep trying; experts say it can take twelve to fifteen tries before a kid will accept new taste sensations and flavors. Yeah, we know it's rough; we do. We know the whining is miserable. Our point is this: Don't give up because your food offerings get rejected. Your ego should be stronger than that, and it's your job as a parent to continue to provide strong boundaries. Try it. Your message should be loud and clear and unchanging: "You don't have to eat it all; you just need to give it a chance."

NO TRICKS OR DISGUISES ALLOWED

Loads of things make us crazy: comb-overs on bald men, useless (often pantless) starlets getting publicity, overpaid professional athletes, and faux cooks/cookbook writers who give you recipes to disguise vegetables for kids.

Hell, no. This is just not right. Trust is elemental. No tricking them into anything.

More to the point—vegetables are delicious.

Discard the old wives' tales and prejudices about what kids will or will not eat. Just because *you* may not like something or weren't exposed to it doesn't mean that your kid won't like it, or shouldn't be given the opportunity to be a hater. Period.

They're entitled to their likes and dislikes just as you are, but—trust us on this one—you just need to keep trying. Offer food neutrally. Keep offering it. No games or gimmicks or disguises. We had one child who would steal broccoli off her sister's plate, which was a good redistribution of food, because her sister hated the stuff. The broccoli hater had a thing for peppers and would come home from school and beg for roasted peppers in garlic and olive oil on whole-wheat baguettes for a snack.

One kid even had a thing for arugula and Bibb lettuce. Desperately homesick at summer camp, she compiled a crafty plea for early release. Topping her list of injustices? The camp served only *iceberg lettuce*.

We recently witnessed a gaggle of three-year-olds exposed to Brussels sprouts for the first time. They received no parental cues about what their response should be. And what did most of them do? Wolfed down the whole plate and asked for seconds.

FOOD SWAPPING

FROM L.A. TO Albany, people are cooking food in batches and sharing. Organize your own "swap" with friends. Divvy up proteins, veggies, and grains, and let their cooking enliven your dinner menu. Save money going out. Save time preparing different foods. This may be just the recipe to lighten your load.

WHAT IS "BABY FOOD," ANYWAY?

Why buy premade processed baby food? It's costly and can never be as good as homemade. Roasting sweet potatoes to go with the chicken and green beans? Grab the blender or food processor, take the skin off the potatoes, and process them. Take the meat from the chicken—grind it up. Green beans. Ditto.

Our kid's first finger food? Cubes of tiny tofu cooked in chicken broth.

Do you really need to buy them special tubes of Sesame Street yogurt? No. We bought big containers of plain yogurt or kefir, bananas, strawberries, blueberries, mangoes, etc., and asked them which fruit they wanted us to blend into special drinks. We filled up sippy cups and watched them guzzle. It's fun, better for them, better for your wallet, and better for the environment.

BUY BY THE CASE

LOOK, WE'RE BIG believers in preservative-free, organic products for your tots. We're also—we swear—realists. Prepared food may be the simplest way to feed them the healthy stuff, as long as you buy organic. Which one? There are many on the market, but we're big fans of Plum Organics' mission and products.

To save dough, watch for sales and then buy by the case.

Save time and money by processing batches of food and freezing them in trays or individual containers, then reheat them in the microwave. So easy. So cheap. Best of all, you have control over what goes into your little tot's diet.

STRAIGHT FROM THE SOURCE

OUR LOVE OF food comes directly from our mom. She was an amazing cook and eater who never met a roadside farmers' market she didn't love. Her mom grew up on a dairy farm, and her dad owned a restaurant, so she came honestly to her food obsession.

In our family, as one meal ended, conversation turned to the next one: "The beets in the market are on sale and gorgeous—I'm going to make borscht for Sunday dinner," or "The butcher told me they just got in veal; he'll have a breast for me when he finishes butchering the fancy cuts. I'll stuff it for Thursday." In all honesty we were picky. The idea of eating veal, let alone a stuffed breast, was disgusting and worthy of boycott. At other times we dramatically exited the house at the smell of liver cooking. Even so, we look back with nostalgia at those days, at that attitude of practical excitement, that connection to growers and salespeople. She was a true and passionate "foodie."

There were five of us kids, and chaos reigned. We didn't have much dough to go around, and we all helped in the kitchen preparing and then cleaning up after meals. Our mom was a serious cook, in the old-school way. Frozen foods, canned veggies, and packaged products didn't often make it into the pantry.

We also watched our fair share of television, particularly Saturday morning cartoons. Only two foods were so appealing that we ever begged for them: boxes of cereals (not the cereal, per se; like kids everywhere what we wanted was the flimsy toy surprise) and frozen TV dinners. But those dinners were really expensive—pricier to buy five packages for five mouths than to make a roast for dinner. But on very rare occasions, Mom caved, bought Swanson frozen chicken dinners, and would telegraph her distaste with a crinkled nose when asked why she wasn't joining us.

We'd set up the folding TV tables (a vestige of another era, before television sets and computer screens invaded every kitchen) and plant ourselves in front of the television to watch *Star Trek.*

When we ate those TV dinners it was like we'd left our country or were lost in space eating foreign foods.

They tasted nothing like the roast chicken she made, or the applesauce that went through the old Foley mill, or the green beans that came from the garden, or the hand-mashed potatoes with butter and cream. But, man, we loved those dinners in the aluminum trays. They were salty and sweet and greasy. The potatoes tasted like cardboard—but in a novel and good way. The applesauce was a thick amber gloss and syrupy sweet, the peas gray-green and mushy. The piece of white-meat chicken was dark brown and soggy, but—once you extracted the fatty gristle—utterly delicious. But it wasn't really food. It was like the occasional candy bar, or made-for-astronauts dehydrated ice cream, or cotton candy at the amusement park.

Our point? We grew up eating real food. Homemade food that was not expensive, packaged, and processed. It was simply prepared, lovingly seasoned, and delicious. Our palates knew the difference between the good stuff and the junk.

19

REFINING YOUR ATTITUDE:
Sugar and Sweets
and Snacks, Oh, My!

We're human beings, not holier-than-thou martyrs. We don't believe in carob instead of chocolate; we don't believe in "low-fat" ice cream. We believe that excess in anything is not good for anyone, but demonizing cakes and candy is not serving anyone. Sweets, snacks, and a little junk have a place in every home. Make them yourself and you'll have more appreciation for their deliciousness—and we believe the more time spent cooking, the less time spent eating. You'll demystify the "treat" aspect, the forbidden-fruit aspect, and eliminate the yucky-nasty-preservatives aspect. And it's way cheaper than buying them at the store.

WHO INVENTED DESSERT, ANYWAY?

Our other sweet memory of home is freshly baked pies and coffee cakes that always seemed to be waiting for us in the kitchen.

There was nothing better than coming home after a long day at school, having a square of warm cake fresh from the Pyrex baking dish along with a glass of milk, and talking at the kitchen table about our day. And, believe it or not, many a day we would pass on cake or brownies in favor of apples we had picked at the farm or plums we had grown in the backyard. Our all-time favorite treat? Way too expensive to have very often—dried apricots, pretzels, and rarely available bottles of 7UP.

We never had dessert at dinner. We never asked. It just never occurred to anyone that that was when you ate a sweet.

STAND FIRM

Oh, and this is as good a place as any to remind you that a good mom never, ever uses food as a reward or punishment. Period.

SODA ROT

YES, WE LOVED occasional sips of 7UP as a kid. But we're here to say that very little on the food landscape rivals the empty nutrition of soda. Oh, you say, just skip the high-fructose corn syrups and go for the diet crap? Don't. Artificial sweeteners suck, too. God only knows what a long life of drinking them will do to your kiddos. And if that doesn't give you pause, studies implicate carbonated beverages with phosphoric acid in contributing to bone loss. Like you or your kids need that!

That said, we do like fizzy stuff. Consider buying club soda or seltzer water and adding pureed fresh fruit to make homemade drinks. Fun, creative, and way better for all concerned.

The best choice for a health-conscious, budget-minded mom? Water.

FORBIDDEN FRUIT AND OTHER SNACKS

We remember the first day we were the parent helper at our three-year-old daughter's nursery school. We were more than a little intimidated by the officious director who felt the need to sit in the back to monitor our monitoring the three-year-olds. The two cardinal rules at this place: no guns and no sugar. (The high-minded parents at this school liked to talk about trade, imperialism, world war, and how sugar-eating, gun-playing toddlers might unwittingly conform to the dominant hegemony— Well, you get the gist of it.) A toy gun was to be instantly confiscated, and a child using two fingers to simulate a gun was to be taken aside and redirected to a more wholesome activity and, if that didn't work, given a time-out. Even though this sounded a little controlling to us, we had no boys in our house and no experience in managing what were obviously homicidal little ruffians. We would cooperate.

The other stern rule: no sugar in any of the snacks brought in to be shared. Ever. Period. Nada.

But on that very first morning, we found ourselves in the middle of a craft project that involved a five-pound yellow bag of Domino sugar at the center of the table. As the kids measured and poured directly out of that huge bag, sugar ended up everywhere. We turned our backs for a split second to get a broom and turned around to find ten crazed, wild-eyed, hysterical tots licking sugar off the floors, off the tables, off the chairs, off our daughter. She burst out crying.

Moral of the story: We know refined sugar in excess is bad. Equally bad? Sugar deprivation. Unless you want a scene out of a tiny-tot vampire horror flick.

SMART SNACKS ARE NOT SNACKWELL'S

Being a smart eater and smart snack provider are synonymous with being a smart mom on a budget. Your trade here is a little sweat equity and a lot of flexibility.

We know the problem of sending your kid to school with a wax Baggie of homemade goodness for their midmorning bite. It's just not sexy. The kid next to her has the latest Pixar movie characters emblazoned on her package of sweetened reformulated faux-gurt. The boy across from her has a crunchy granola bar loaded with extra sugar and fat. And her best friend has organic salted barbecue chips. Not only is your daughter now the least cool kid in the class, but the other stuff looks so much better.

It is not a failure of your parenting skill that she doesn't have enough self-esteem to rejoice in her wax Baggie filled with a home-baked 100 percent whole-wheat zucchini muffin that is—let's be honest here—an unappealing green and brown. Think of this as part of your success. . . . After all, she's aware of her social milieu, wants to fit in, and is a normal kid enticed by shiny bells and whistles.

What's a mom to do?

Give in sometimes. Buy her those organic bags of potato chips and the occasional gummy-goo gizmos every kid craves. (We can't believe some of the things our kids took. Ugh!)

Then work with her to figure out what you can make at home (better for the wallet) that is socially acceptable, appealing to her eye (better to fit in), and made with good ingredients (better for her health). You've got the veggies cut and ready to go; just add a dip like peanut butter or hummus. Concoct your own homemade granola or flavored organic popcorn. Fill a container with plain yogurt topped with fresh coconut, strawberries, mango. . . .

TURN OFF THE FAT FOOD NETWORK

WE'RE ALL FOR family food entertainment. We watch the twisted sadism of Gordon Ramsay on *Hell's Kitchen* with a mix of awe and horror. We've spent seasons invested in *Top Chef* and *Chopped*. Love Lidia and Ming on PBS. And, of course, nothing rivals a good Julia and Pierre rerun fest. But as food worshipers we cringe at what the Food Network has become. From the once all Emeril, all the time to the mostly Bobby, all the time, the network has morphed into a bunch of fat pushers supported by Big Agra selling the most disgusting packaged and prepared food products ever. It's not only that the shows glorify really bad food habits. But if we see one more promo for that guy going into a diner and delighting in the greasy deli and dogs, we will throw something at the television.

THE JUNK FOOD DRAWER

Okay. We're about to get into trouble with the healthy food police, every nutritional expert in the world . . . even ourselves! But we're big believers in keeping some junk around. This is predicated, of course, on the pantry and refrigerator being filled with great food. While muumuu-clad little ones is not the goal, you can't shelter them from everything. They need to experience, learn, and be able to self-regulate when they go into the big cruel Mickey D world. Besides, who are we kidding? Some of that crap tastes really good—every kid should be able to have a Snickers bar sometimes.

PART 4

SMART MAMAS ARE SMART ABOUT MONEY:

Get Control of Your Finances
(and Pass It On)

INTRODUCTION

We've lured you in talking about cute clothes and yummy food, but it's time to get right to the heart of the issue. Because, sure, you can learn to be a smart shopper, you can save dough here and there, but until you get your budgets in order, introduce money into family conversation, and teach your children how to have a healthy relationship with all things financial, you're not really being a smart mom.

So. A few questions:

Is your financial house in absolutely perfect order? Are you confident about your budgets? Do you have clear financial plans? Do you save for emergencies, retirement, college?

If so, we're willing to wager that your closets are pin-neat, shirts and pants hanging by color and style; your kitchen counters are sparkling; your hair is immaculate; and your manicured nails never dare to chip. In other words, we're betting you don't exist.

Come on. No one is all that.

And no one is totally comfortable talking about money.

Freedom, opportunity, comfort, security, power, control, frustration, fear are all dispensed at the money machine. How do we earn it? Who has riches? Who doesn't have a dime? How much do we really need? How do we manage what we have or, as the case may be, what we *don't* have? Let's be honest: Money worries of some form permeate the air of every household. If you're reading this book, you've got 'em. And just like you're the most important influence on your kids when it comes to dressing and eating, you're also their model when it comes to learning good money habits.

Remember in everything we do and say, we pass on our values to our kiddos. Often this happens subtly, insidiously, without our conscious thought. Money is no exception. What message are you sending when you're shoving unopened bills into the drawer or trash? Or when you implore your little tyke not to tell Daddy about that impulsive shoe purchase at the mall? (Yes, we know: You're racked by guilt, but how could you resist? They were obscenely cute.) Or when you're gossiping with your friends about the rich guy down the street who dates all those hot young things.

Your kids are listening. They're watching.

Take a vow today: to find financial stability by getting your own house in order, to take responsibility for teaching your children about (all kinds of) dough, and to integrate money sense into your family's daily life.

20

FINDING FINANCIAL SAFETY

YOU'RE NOT DOOMED TO REPEAT IT

Growing up, did your family talk about money openly, clearly, in a mindful, nonanxious way? Uh, we haven't met many people who can say yes.

How *was* money discussed in your home? Were there contentious debates about the household budget? Were there recriminations about one person's spending? Hushed or noisy anxiety about debt? Envious observations about what others had, drove, or wore?

Or was yours a house where money wasn't to be discussed? Maybe your parents wanted to shield you from their financial worries, or maybe they felt it was tacky to discuss their abundant moola. Either way, no one ever talked about where money came from or how things were paid for, and here you are today wondering why you can't get the hang of this budget thing.

Like it or not, how you grew up shapes how you live today.

The money messages you did (or didn't) receive are probably the same ones you're sharing (or failing to share) with your kids. So come to terms with your own money legacy. Think about the messages you want your kids to hear. Be mindful. Be clear. Educate your kids the way you weren't educated. Got it? Good.

"BUDGET" IS NOT A DIRTY WORD

Next step: Look carefully at your current financial reality and start to budget today.

Today? Yes, you heard correctly. Today. Right now. A clear idea of your resources, your expenses, and your future will let you plan ahead and enjoy living in the moment. This isn't going to increase your take-home pay, but by having clear boundaries (everyone needs 'em) you'll all sleep better at night.

EQUAL SAY FOR ALL (ALMOST)

Money equals conflict.

Why do countries fight? Resources and control: oil, water, a crown. Why do siblings fight? Resources and control: parental love, toys, the TV remote. Why do married couples and partners fight? Resources and control: spending, sex, the last word.

Now think of money as the barter unit that represents an exchange of resources (product or service). The single biggest source of friction between partners is money. Imagine if you could find a way to reduce the rub over allocation and control of your family resources. Wouldn't there be a lot less scrapping?

You need to work on and set up budgets, together. No fighting. No name-calling. No martinis to numb the pain. (Well, maybe one.) By doing this together you'll be forced to agree on priorities, to have a healthy give-and-take on how you share your resources, and to come to some thoughtful decisions on what you value (football tix versus violin lessons; mani-pedis versus dinners out; camping trips versus boutique hotels).

Age-appropriate, family budget discussions are valuable lessons for your kids, too, helping them learn basic money skills, how to plan, and how to compromise.

OPEN YOUR EYES AND BALANCE THE BOOKS

The simplest place to start getting organized is online. If you're not already using an electronic program like Quicken or Microsoft Money to manage your accounts, you need to start. Better yet, we're devoted disciples of Mint.com and Yodlee.com (not as slick and glossy but every bit as sharp) as one-stop budget and investment account organizers. Both are simple tools that help you keep track of your assets and liabilities, set up a budget, make payments, and balance your checkbook.

LINE-ITEM VETO

YES, WE *DID* *say* balance your checkbook. We're shocked by how many people don't. While you can go online to see what your balance is and which checks have cleared, you're never totally in control. Banks make mistakes (duh, like you haven't already witnessed this?). We're talking basic record keeping. We're talking a way to compare expenses month-to-month, year-to-year, so you can begin to account for your life.

SMART MONEY RESOURCES

Does This Make My Assets Look Fat? by Susan L. Hirshman

Can I Retire? by Michael R. Piper

Ask for It by Linda Babcock and Sara Laschever

LearnVest: www.learnvest.com

Suze Orman: www.suzeorman.com

Manisha Thakor: manishathakor.com/

Your first task? A macroexamination of your income, assets (things you own), and liabilities (things you owe), and an assessment of your future financial needs. Then you'll start tracking on a microlevel all the ways you spend money: from the latte at the coffee shop to the third pair of mittens Susie just had to have to the gas expenses. We bet you'll be shocked at how much goes down the tube at CVS and Walgreens and how much gets eaten up dining out.

THE MACRO LOOK: HOME AGAIN, HOME AGAIN

Housing will be at the top of your expense list. Then will likely come transportation, food, utilities, debt repayment (toe tapping—we're not happy about this if the words "credit card" are anywhere involved), clothing, entertainment, insurance, savings, and so on. An overview of your complete financial picture lets you make better decisions. For example, when you see the bite your housing expenses take from your overall budget, you might finally decide to move to the less expensive, up-and-coming town you've been flirting with. Or maybe you'll decide that your commute into the city from an out-of-the-way place is actually costly to your budget. All along you thought it would save you money, but a closer examination shows that owning and running two cars (with car payments, gas, maintenance, insurance, and parking) is prohibitive. It may very well be that the quality of life for your entire family will improve with less space and more convenient access to work, allowing you more time with your family, a diverse community, and closer access to cultural activities. Long-held beliefs about money often get turned on their head once the numbers are on paper.

Trust us, the one thing that happens to young and growing families is that all the acts of daily living—earaches, soccer practice, broken limbs, getting dinner on the table, homework crises, aging parents, work trauma—prevent you from closely examining the way that you *are* living. Doing a budget is about far more than the money; think of it as an annual opportunity to take stock of the value of your lifestyle.

UH-OH MOBILE

We talked a lot in *Bitches on a Budget* about cars and auto-related expenses. To sum it up, new cars just aren't worth it. If you need wheels, buy used, and buy fuel efficient; new cars depreciate 45 percent within the first three years. Even greater savings can be realized through carpooling and public transit (if it's convenient and fits your schedule). But we'll be real. We know busy moms must think about practicality above all else. So we can talk about taking the train until we're blue in the face, but if it's not feasible, you won't do it. Say you need to be at day care by five o'clock or Jamie becomes a ward of the state. Say you'd love to get the exercise and be a good green mama running errands on your bike, but Kaly, Kendra, Jake, and the dog don't fit on the fenders. We understand. Our only beef? People who drive massive, gas-guzzling vehicles and then complain about the cost. Scale down. A safe, efficient vehicle is better for your budget— and better for the earth those kiddos are inheriting.

A PENNY SAVED IS A PENNY SAVED

Are you sitting down? We're recommending you take an immediate 20 percent pay cut.

Huh?

Honey, this is about being smart with your money, taking care of your kiddos, and taking care of yourself. The smartest move you can make? Take 10 percent off the top for current savings, and 10 percent more for retirement savings.

Why do this?

Once you have savings you have control over your life. You will reduce your daily anxiety and insecurity. You'll be ahead of the game. You'll be able to actually look forward to the pleasurable ways you'll be able to use that money, whether it's renovating the kitchen or sending Sam to Spain to study Spanish.

Besides, nothing is certain in life. You may have the best job in the world today and lose it tomorrow. You may be healthy today and not tomorrow. Your furnace may break down, your refrigerator crap out, your roof spring a leak. Savings will let you weather the storm.

WAYS TO MICROTRACK EXPENSES

First, the old-fashioned way: a pencil and paper recording each transaction or an envelope that catches every receipt for all purchases. This can be tough for a busy mom with a household of rug rats underfoot.

· Another idea? Use a credit card for all purchases: groceries, utility payments, dentist trips. Your credit card (or the online programs linked to it) should automatically categorize payments by type of expense or give you the tools to do so. Our Whole Foods bills go into the same category as our Stop & Shop bills. All the gas and car repair—related expenses are aggregated. Easy to keep track of everything.

We also like this because our credit card accrues air miles. Other friends have credit cards that give cash back.

Warning: This method is only for the mature mamas in the house—those committed to and capable of paying off their balance every month. Never, ever use your credit card to finance daily living. Meaning if you use it for all purchases, you *must pay it off every month.* No good will ever come of racking up credit card debt (see "Plastic Is Explosive," page 167). If you don't have the control to responsibly use plastic, stay away.

EASY-PEASY

PAY ALL BILLS online. Lots of folks don't like to, but we've taken the leap. Although we admit to a few small, tiny little errors, like a single keystroke payment of $11,187 to the electric company instead of $118.70. Ah, details. Paying online is a time saver, and with automatic payments made for recurring expenses, you won't damage your credit rating or incur a penalty by forgetting the due date. (See page 225 for security if you're online in a public place.)

21

PRACTICAL ADVICE FOR EVERY MAMA:
Insurance, College, Tax Credits, Retirement, Plastic, and Better Sex

Okay, we'll admit that "better sex" was just to get you to keep reading. These are topics that make our eyes glaze over. But the peace of mind you'll get from taking care of these things may very well improve your sex life. So bear with us.

DEATH

Perhaps the only taboo subject that rivals sex and money is death. Most people don't invest as much energy getting their affairs in order as they do praying for eternal salvation. Yet you need to. Make a will; select guardians for your children; appoint an executor; do a review of your insurance policies. The peace of mind you'll find will—we promise—enhance your life, help you relax, and, hopefully, bring you and your partner together in all sorts of exciting ways.

WHAT'S OURS IS OURS.
What's Mine Is Mine.

IF YOU'RE A married mama, let's make a few things perfectly clear. 1: You should participate in all financial decisions with your spouse. 2: You should have a list of all your financial accounts and know the location of all your financial documents. (You should do this married or not, of course.) 3: You should have a credit card account in your own name. You need a credit history. We've heard horror stories of women either divorced or widowed who, in moments of great trauma, struggle to establish credit in their own names.

If you're at home taking care of the house and the kids, value your work. Too often, women at home don't feel entitled to participate in money decisions. This is antediluvian. You are contributing. You are working. Honor yourself and value your work—in a monetary way.

WHOM WILL YOU TRUST?

Wills and trusts are not just for millionaires. Imagine something were to happen to you. Who would take care of your children? What would happen to your house? If you don't think about this ahead of time, you leave it up to family members, the courts (ugh), and chance to make those decisions.

While you've got your wits, spend time thinking about who shares your family values, and whom you trust to love and raise your children. Yes, this is horrible to contemplate, so many of us don't. But hiding and denying don't make this responsibility go away. Pick a guardian or guardians for your children.

Do you have a bank account, a house, and a life insurance

policy? Without a will, your heirs will end up in court to sort this out. Even if your assets are not huge, you need someone to manage your estate, so you must appoint an executor. We advise making the executor a different person from the guardian.

Now that you're organized, tell the person you've appointed as executor where to find a master list of all your possessions of value and all your accounts.

Depending on the size of your estate, it might make sense from a tax perspective to have some of the assets protected in trust. We're often confused by legalese and feel comforted when someone puts it into simple language, so we like to consult with a living, breathing lawyer person. You may be fine working online. Look into Rocket Lawyer and LegalZoom.

INCREASE DEDUCTIBLES AND SAVE

CAREFULLY LOOK AT your deductibles in case of loss on both home and auto. Ask your insurer to do a schedule of the cost of insurance with a $250, $500, and $1,000 deductible. Raising deductibles may save you big money—but you've got to then be prepared to shell out in the event of a claim. If you're prone to fender-benders or ice dams, this may not work. But many of us go years between claims, and it's worth the risk to increase the deductibles and save on the annual premium.

CAR AND HOME INSURANCE

Everyone with a home mortgage must have insurance; the banks demand it. This policy will insure both the dwelling and the contents. Want more? Whether you're a renter or a home owner, look into an umbrella liability insurance policy that protects you whether someone falls down your steps and sues you or you accidentally hurt someone *outside* of your home. While your home owners' or auto insurance will cover some of this kind of liability, it's limited, and if you have assets that someone could sue you for, save them by having this kind of protection.

If you're a renter, look into getting a policy to cover the cost of replacing your possessions if you're the victim of a theft or a fire. Closely examine your car coverage as well. It may be that your car is old enough that it no longer pays to have collision coverage.

TAKE A RISK ON A NEW INSURER

- Compare prices.
- Every three to five years shop around.
- If you find a lower rate but you're happy where you are, ask your insurer to match it—often they will.
- Don't blindly take the word of your friendly neighborhood agent. Read the fine print. Insist on several competing quotes.
- Investigate the company by going to *Consumer Reports*, the attorney general's Consumer Protection Division, or the Better Business Bureau.
- Amica Mutual Insurance, USAA (if you have a military connection), and Chubb all get high marks.

LIFE INSURANCE: WHOLE VERSUS TERM LIFE

What if something happens to you? If you're a working mom and your family depends on your income, how would they pay the rent or mortgage? If you're an at-home mom, how would your spouse pay for great child care? If something happens to your partner, how would you maintain your standard of living? Time to talk about life insurance.

The question is, what kind of insurance should you get: term life or universal life (whole, universal, variable)? Confused? It's actually pretty simple: With term you pay an annual fee and, if you die, your family gets a cash death payout. Universal plans are a combination of insurance and an investment account.

Unless you're wealthy and there are estate-planning advantages, we can see no reason for you to buy a universal policy. They are more expensive than term plans. While there is forced saving, the fees associated with these accounts are not worth the return. You are better off being a disciplined saver in a no-load mutual stock or bond fund.

SMART MAMA TIP:
Make Friends with the Competition

WE'RE ALWAYS NAGGING you to shop around and compare, to embrace the snarly consumer inside you. Often, though, we don't know what we don't know (actually, that's true about 90 percent of living) and don't find out what we *should* have known until it's too late. Who better to fill you in on the fine print and all the little things you should be looking for than someone's competitor? So, when you're shopping around, ask companies to compare and contrast their service and their competitor's. For example, "I'm talking to Joe Blow about the rider for frozen pipe replacement. What do you offer that Joe Blow doesn't? What are things that you do better? What are they missing? What's in their fine print that I should be wary of?"

THE COLLEGE INVESTMENT

There is nothing richer or more soul satisfying than learning, and every mom wants her kids to get the best education they can. Studies repeatedly show that the higher the level of education a kid gets, the higher his/her lifetime earning power.

The question, of course, is how to pay for it. Today, top-tier private college tuition and expenses are in the $40-to-$50K-range per year, and your kids are probably still little. Hard to imagine what the expenses will be when they go to college, right? Feeling heart palpitations yet?

In today's dollars, sending Emily to Harvard could top $200K. The good news is that the most elite colleges and universities will find a way for your little Einstein to go without tremendous financial hardships for the family. The bad news is that there are only a handful of these schools and very few admission slots for those with, or without, the means to pay.

Yes, we believe you: Your kids are geniuses. But you can't predict whether Fran (who is now five and expert at singing rounds of "Row, Row, Row Your Boat" while splashing in the tub) will get a full ride on a crew scholarship to Duke. You can't be sure that Maria (ten and a Homer fanatic) will be the last young woman on earth with a gift for dead classical languages, thus guaranteeing her sponsorship by the Ancient Greek department anxious to fill seats and keep its program funded. Jeff may be the best pitcher in his age group all the way through eleventh grade, recruited by U of A on a full ride, only to throw out his back (and scholarship) horsing around with friends in the fall of his senior year.

Blindly hoping your kid's rare talent will result in a full scholarship somewhere—rather than saving and thinking shrewdly about education—is a recipe for disaster.

NO PARENTS ALLOWED
(Only Their Money)

ONE OF THE great ironies of the college years is that most schools have no contact with parents regarding their children. Yes, you'll get invited to visiting weekend—but, honey, let's be honest: These are "development" (aka pocket-picking) opportunities, not evidence that the school wants you involved in your kid's life. Hey, we think that's healthy, and we really don't mind that they don't send their report cards home to you anymore. Yet when it comes to paying for college, they are looking to *you* to pay.

THE COLLEGE FUND

One strategy is to sock away money each month. But with interest rates low and the stock market gyrating, there is no simple answer on which savings vehicle you should be using. One option is a 529 plan. Simply put, these are investment plans that allow you to put away money and have it grow federal-income-tax-free (sometimes state-tax-free as well) when it is withdrawn and used to pay for their college tuition. Some states offer a version of this plan that allows you to prepay and lock in tuition at today's rates.

EDUCATE YOURSELF

FOR MORE INFORMATION on prepaid tuition and college savings plans, start here:

College Savings Plans Network: www.collegesavings.org

U.S. Securities and Exchange Commission: www.sec.gov/ investor

FinAid: www.finaid.org

Morningstar ratings for 529 plans by state: http:// 529.morningstar.com/state-map.action

A mama caution: *Read the fine print!* Some plans are safer than others. Just because it's through a state agency doesn't mean the funds are guaranteed.

As of this writing, you can contribute up to $13,000 per year to each child's fund. If you have the extra money (remember, funding your retirement should come first), this is one smart way to begin saving for college. Just be aware that you cannot use the money for anything other than college payments without paying a penalty. But the money can go to anyone's college tuition. So let's say you're earmarking the fund for Maria, but she takes off for Delphi with that cute Greek dude. Well, if Fran doesn't get that rowing scholarship, the funds can be used for Fran.

GET CREDIT WHERE CREDITS ARE DUE

FLEXIBLE SPENDING ACCOUNTS

Many companies, including the federal government (one of the world's largest employers), offer a benefit called a flexible spending account that covers certain medical and dependent care (child care/dependent adult care) costs. If you're among the one in four Americans eligible for these plans, be certain to take advantage. This benefit allows you to contribute pretax dollars to an account your employer oversees and manages.

What makes this a terrific plan is that you are using pretax dollars to pay for your otherwise uncovered expenses. What makes this tricky is that if you don't use what you've banked, you lose it. For example, let's say you anticipate $3,500 in expenses for uncovered deductibles (doctor-visit copays, eyeglasses for your husband, orthodontia for Lauren, Ativan for you), but you have a particularly healthy and stress-free year and use only $2,800 of that amount. Your employer gets to keep the $700 left in the account. Suddenly you need that Ativan. Plan carefully.

DEPENDENT-CARE FLEXIBLE SPENDING ACCOUNT

The dependent-care flexible spending account works just like the FSA for medical expenses: Use it or lose it. In order to qualify, your employer needs to offer it; your kids need to be under thirteen; the money must be spent on care so the parent(s) can work. (If you are the caregiver of a disabled or elderly person, you should also be looking into taking this credit.) If one of you is a non-income-producing parent, unless you are a student or disabled you can't use this benefit—a fact that should really piss off stay-at-home moms—or dads. What do they think SAHMs are doing, eating bonbons?

You can put aside up to $5,000 per year if you are married and filing a joint return, or if you are a single parent. If you are married and filing separately, you can fund this account up to $2,500 dollars. (Be careful that you and your spouse are on the same page when you make this election at work and do not overfund this account. It is nonrefundable.) This can be used for day care, summer day camp, and nanny and babysitter expenses. Remember, though, that to collect this benefit you need to report the caregiver's Social Security information. (For more detailed information consult this IRS publication: http://www.irs.gov/pub/irs-pdf/i2441.pdf.)

Again, you need to plan carefully. Remember: Use it or lose it.

CHILD AND DEPENDENT CARE CREDIT

Unlike an FSA, which is available only through a place of employment, the Child Care Credit (not to be confused with the Child Tax Credit) option is open to everyone. Like the FSA, though, it benefits only to the full extent of the reported income of the lowest household earner (except if that person is a student or disabled). The Child Care Credit will cover up to $3,000 in expenses for one child, and up to $6,000 for two or more. You may receive credit for up to 35 percent of your qualifying expenses. If you are the caregiver of a disabled or elderly person, this is another credit you should look into. (For more detailed information consult this IRS publication: http://www.irs.gov/pub/irs-pdf/p503.pdf.)

Don't get caught in "Nannygate"! If you're using either the Child Care Credit or FSA as tax deductions, you must state whom you are paying for this care and she must report the income on her tax return. If a caregiver is employed by you to work in your home, you must report this on your tax forms and may be responsible for paying Social Security and unemployment taxes on that individual.

So which one? It's really confusing. If you're eligible for

both, you'll need to crunch the tax numbers to find the right fit for your financial situation. (See http://www.bls.gov/opub/cwc/cm20070321ar01p1.htm.)

SECTION 132 (SOUNDS LIKE SOMETHING OUT OF A KEN KESEY NOVEL, NO?)

ANOTHER FSA TYPE of account (but this one doesn't expire) is part of the Transportation Equity Act for the Twenty-first Century. It allows you to set aside money—again in those rocking pretax dollars—for transportation expenses. As of this writing, the maximum per month you can set aside for mass transit or parking is $230.

INTEREST(ING)—SORT OF

WHAT'S THE DIFFERENCE between simple and compounding interest and why should I care?

Simple interest calculates on the original amount only. So if you borrowed or invested $1,000 and the interest rate was 5 percent, after one year you would have or owe $1,050; after five years you would have or owe $1,500; and after thirty years you would have or owe $2,500.

Compound interest takes the original amount and calculates the interest rate *including the amount that has been added*.

Year 1 = $1,050. Year 10 = $1,628.89. Year 30 = $4,321.94.

As you can see, in the short term there's not a huge difference, but over time it adds up. Look closely at interest rates on both saving (which is when we love compounding) and borrowing (don't love compounding).

PLASTIC IS EXPLOSIVE

Compounding interest on credit-card debt can ruin you. A simple rule: Pay off your bills each month. Period. Otherwise, you're on the slippery path to indebtedness. If you're in trouble with your credit cards, now is the time to stop, take a deep breath, and work out a plan to begin paying them off.

For most of us, a plastic card is a plastic card. They all look the same. Red, blue, white, green—what's the difference, and should my kids have them?

- A *credit card* allows you to revolve your balance by paying a minimum amount each month. Interest rates are remarkably high (at this writing one of the AmEx cards we researched charged as much as 19 percent APR interest).

- A *charge card* usually requires an annual fee, has no credit limit, and requires you to pay off your balance at the end of the month. If you do not pay off your bill at the end of each month the penalty incurred is high. We see no reason for you to pay for a charge card.

- A *debit card* automatically deducts cash from your checking account. A great tool for kids once they are navigating around town on their own. If you set up an account like this for your child, establish a no-overdraft policy with the bank (actually you should do this for yourself, too).

- A *prepaid card* is one you fully fund up front. They often come with ridiculously high hidden fees and do not offer the purchase protection you get with regular credit cards. Unless you're on the lam or trying to rebuild a damaged credit history, there is no reason to use them. Don't.

NOT ALL PLASTIC IS CREATED EQUAL

TAKE THE TIME to compare your current card's interest rates and reward programs with others. For a one-stop comparison of cards check Nerdwallet.com or Cardhub.com or CardRatings.com. In addition, read multiple resources before you select one. Rates vary and the fine print is tricky. So do your homework.

PLASTIC FOR KIDS

Once your kids start earning their own babysitting or lawn-mowing money, help them get an ATM card tied to a new savings account. This will allow them to deposit and withdraw their own earnings. Just make sure this account has no overdraft privileges—banks are evil and make huge amounts of money on overdraft fees—and it is separate from any "big" savings account they may have in their name. As soon as our kids started driving we linked their ATM debit cards to a credit card so that they had access to funds in case of an emergency. This debit account's credit-card feature had a capped spending limit. (A very small limit.) When they left the house for college (yes, mamas, that day does come), we helped them get their first credit card by opening a joint account with them. Once they learned how to be responsible for paying monthly bills, they got a credit card in just their name; this was the first step in establishing their own credit history.

SAVE TO RETIRE

Experts counsel that you should put 10 percent of your pretax income into some sort of retirement fund. We know what you're thinking: *What, save money for me? My kids need school supplies and they're begging to go to Disney!* Ladies, this is like being on the plane when the oxygen masks deploy: Put it around your face first and then help those in need. We can't say this loudly enough. So many young mamas don't have the time to even realize they aren't taking care of themselves. You *must* plan for your future.

Despite the 6.2 percent that comes out of your paycheck each month, Social Security was not designed to fully fund you in retirement. It was built as a safety net and a supplemental means of income. Besides, given the budget deficit and the aging population, do not delude yourself for a minute that Sam is going to be holding your hand in the old-age home, for he's no longer a rich uncle. No one but you can take care of you. (Well, maybe Junior, if he becomes more financially savvy than you are because you've taught him money smarts.)

22

CENTS AND SENSIBILITY

Now that you're financially savvy mamas, it's time to teach your kids how money works. It's up to you to show them that money doesn't grow on trees or inside cash machines. It's up to you to give them the critical tools they need to become responsible consumers, savers, and investors.

We live in a consumer-driven economy that depends on increasing consumption year after year. The drive to buy is embedded in everything we read, watch, and do, and it's your job to teach your kids to carefully read the messages the media is sending, as opposed to getting caught by emotional hooks. To be smart money managers, they must be savvy media decoders and skeptical consumers. And since wanton consumption (sounds like a new dish) is often a substitute for real gratification, you need to help your kids distinguish between needs and wants.

This is not easy.

Humans are curious by nature. Being interested in new things is part of our DNA. This is a good thing—when channeled constructively. While a tot is thrilled by a block game that teaches shapes, a grade-schooler by a first look at Mars through a telescope, and a teenager by the latest, greatest cell phone, their interest isn't likely satisfied by just one. The next new windup toy, computer game, smartphone, etc., is sure to be equally stimulating. Now add the great persuasive forces of the marketplace. These days, the Don Draper hustler type of the sixties is even better at his craft (though, sadly, not as drop-dead gorgeous) and far more insidious. Today's marketing geniuses are really good at their game—and really bad for you and your kids' financial health.

Be discerning consumers of information so you can teach your kids to do the same. Look critically at all Web sites and blogs: If the site is pitching a story about a product, is there an ad for it on their page, or are they selling the goods they've plugged in the story through an e-commerce portal? Don't trust them. If a television show has hustled you to follow their tweets and sign up to "like" their fan page on Facebook, ask yourself what are you getting from it? NFL Football is selling named gear you can personalize? That's nice, but are they paying you to promote the sport? Help your kids to start noticing what's going on. (See "Advergames" in Part V, "Technomoms.")

THE DIFFERENCE BETWEEN A NEED AND A WANT

In an ideal universe, our needs and our wants would converge. Sometimes this does happen: We need to eat every day to survive, and who doesn't love great food? Often, though, even adoring mothers can get confused between a need and a want. Young kids don't really need much or want more than unconditional love, food, and shelter. They certainly don't "need" Juicy Couture tracksuits (ugh!), Armani Junior shoes, or a Prada diaper bag. Maybe you do, but they don't. (And if you do, why? Keep reading.)

Needs are items that you must have to live: food, shelter, transportation, health care, education, a computer, and, yes, the Internet. *Wants* are all the things that add texture and interest to your basic needs: eating out, white truffles from Italy, vacations, movies, brand-name products, cable.

First of all, help your kids determine why they're asking for something . . . and then drill into whether it is a need or a want. Once there, you can circle back to how this fits into their budgets and the overall family budget. Trust us; you'll save a lot of whining and wheedling if you can effectively get this framework in place.

THE "WHY" DIAGNOSTIC

Q. Ask Lauren whether she wants those gloves because everyone's wearing them.

A. She answers that *all* the girls at school are indeed wearing fingerless gloves and she must have those adorable ones with the faux leopard edging because she wants them, and anyway she needs new gloves.

R. Agree with her that yes, she does need a new pair of gloves, and therefore you will buy her these. Then take this opportunity to discuss doing things just because everyone else is doing them. Talk about the delicate balance between fitting in with your community and just following the herd (see fashion chapter about fitting in).

Q. Ask Sherise if she wants that Nicole by OPI nail color because she read in *People* that Justin Bieber loves the color.

A. Yes, she wants it because Justin Bieber loves it is her simple and honest answer. Of course, she loves it, too.

R. Counsel her that just because a cute Canadian endorses a product, it would be mad to buy it if she doesn't like it, too, and you're relieved to hear she likes it. She is free to spend her allowance on any brand of nail polish she chooses, of course, but remind her that he is making money on the product endorsement.

Q. What is so special about Under Armour that Billy wants that expensive black tee and no other?

A. Billy saw Tom Brady in the Under Armour commercial. He thinks Tom Brady is the best, and the stuff seems so much better than regular no-name tees.

R. You happen to agree that Tommy Terrific is the bomb, but advise Billy that Tommy T. owns a piece of the Under Armour company and gets a cut of the merch each time a tee goes out the door. If he still wants the Under Armour black tee—even though it costs twice as much as the identical product without the label—the up-charge will come out of his allowance or savings.

Think of these moments as the antidote to the drives that propel your kids to want, want, want. Just be careful that you don't become psycho, psychoanalytical killjoys drilling down so deep that you totally frustrate them and they stop talking to you. You'll have lots of other opportunities to drive them to go radio-silent.

A final word on consumption (at least for now): Be careful not to fall into buying them the "best" of everything because you couldn't have it yourself, or because of your need for them to keep up with the kids next door, or because you're afraid to say no. Trust us; if you get into this rut, you lose and they lose.

23

TEACHING MONEY

Money intelligence is an important part of your kids' education and it's a social skill—as critical as "please" and "thank you." You don't expect someone else to teach your kids how to be polite. You shouldn't expect someone else to teach your kids how to manage money.

At every step of the way, your task is to assure them that you are able to and will take care of them, but that money is a scarce commodity and, no, it doesn't grow on trees. Think of it this way: Money is just another resource, like time, that they will need to learn to manage as they navigate through life. So just as you help them with time-management skills—like bedtimes and homework time and online time—you need to help them with money management. There's no moment like when they're young for them to begin learning.

MONEY IS CONTROL

While money gives you control over your life, it should not be used *to control*. This is a critical distinction. Kids should have their own discretionary money starting at a young age. It will help them learn to make choices, and to be responsible for the choices they make. It will give them a feeling of mastery, and they'll be better prepared to manage their own finances when they grow up.

ALLOWANCE IS EMPOWERING

This is as good a place as any to talk about responsibilities and money. We firmly believe that kids need their own agency. No, not the insurance or brokerage kind; we're talking about being independent actors and decision makers who can act on their preferences. Start by giving them a certain amount of money to do with as they please. We do not believe that allowances should be tied to performance. Whether it's cleaning up their room or unloading the dishwasher, there are certain activities you should expect them to participate in as members of the family. No slave labor allowed, but a reasonable plan for chores is wise. Walking the dog after school, setting the table, folding laundry, making beds, leaf raking, snow shoveling. Normal household work. They should do it because they're a part of the family, not because they're getting paid. Allowance should be a predictable, agreed-upon sum, independent from chores.

NO PAY FOR PLAY

AS FAR AS rewarding "high" performance goes, we want to scream and yell and go bonkers every time we hear of a kid getting money for getting an A, or a new iPhone for making the football team. Did your kid do something great? Be a brat and brag to everyone who'll listen. Shower him with praise. Tell him how proud you are. Act like Tom Cruise on the couch with Oprah. But you are *not* allowed to pay them for performance. Uh-uh. This is where doing something because you love it and being loved for who you are (whether benchwarmer or team captain) can get perverted into pay for play. A total and complete mama *fail*.

When your kids are small, start teaching them to separate their dough into buckets—just like you do (right?). We suggest getting them different-colored boxes, piggybanks, even envelopes. Just as you have put away a portion of your money for savings, encourage them to take a portion, say 20 percent, and add it to the savings bucket.

Consider having them put a little aside each week, say 10 percent, for emergency wants. (At their age, saving for emergency needs like a roof repair or root canal seems a little intense; we're thinking replacement iPod when they leave theirs on the bus, or the lift ticket when they can't bear to miss the school ski trip.) We like this because you want them to start to save up for things that are outside of their normal spending range.

Another bucket should be for giving—we'd encourage 10 to 20 percent of their money. While lots of folks will recommend this cash saving go to charity, we prefer tangible acts of charitable giving, particularly for kids. Money remains abstract, and the concrete nature of donating a toy or helping you sort cans at a food bank will be far more instructive and fulfilling for a child. This "giving box" also lets them select and give gifts to family and friends. Besides, when they want to buy you a present, what's worse than having you take them to the store to get it? Having you buy it, too.

No matter their age, make sure you're consistent; give them their allowance on the same day each week. Never make a kid ask you for it. Don't get into the I'll-owe-you or it's-on-your-account rut.

Don't get into the I'll-deduct-it-from-your-allowance rut, either. While you need to be consistent and reliable, they need to be accountable. If they blow their allowance in a day and are short of spending money on the weekend, they have to struggle through. If they make an unwise choice, it's a lesson learned young—and hopefully not repeated on a big scale later.

How much? Everyone lives on a different budget, so this is a question each family must come to on its own. Together, agree to what kids must buy on their own from their allowance. No mysteries. Be clear about your expectations. This is a great time to explore and discuss family values. When do you stop giving them an allowance? Again, this is up to you; we'd say when they are old enough to earn money on their own, whether after school or during the summer.

A CONCRETE JUNGLE

As we move into a paperless and cashless society, the already abstract idea of money becomes even more remote. Think about it: How often do you actually go into a bank and get cash from a teller? How often do you actually count it out? We buy products on the Internet, get groceries delivered, or pay with a debit card at the supermarket. And while it felt weird at the time, we've even swiped our card at the farmers' market.

Young children have a hard enough time with the abstract idea of money—converted into a plastic card or a keystroke, it's nearly impossible to grasp. So it's never too soon to begin teaching the idea of money as a barter unit used in trade for a good or a service. Make it fun. Begin to teach them the idea of exchange, whether it's using a toy cash register to create a restaurant or shop complete with play money and pretend goods, or setting up a movie theater where everyone comes to watch a favorite show and pays for the privilege with chips.

Make it a point to skip the ATM machines and go to the teller to get cash. Count it. Lots of skills can be merged in money mania: counting, sorting, adding, subtracting. Play bank. Really. Teach them the idea of borrowing and lending and interest. Be creative.

As they get older, use real projects to teach them what the difference is between a good and a service. Show them how money borrowed costs money and money invested earns money.

PLAY: USE LEMONS TO MAKE MORE THAN LEMONADE

This is a great tool to teach them about how products come to market and the difference between goods and services. The product will be lemonade—we know, we know, trite and overdone, but it's the perfect choice because it's simple to make and it's easy to assess the cost of goods.

1) THE BANK OF MOMMY

Front your child cash in the form of a business loan to purchase the raw materials: lemons, sugar, and paper cups. Since you're the

Bank of Mommy, you dictate the terms of the loan, just like a bank would. So there will be interest charged on the loan (be generous and keep the calculation simple and age-appropriate: either a flat rate or an easily calculated interest rate, like 1 percent).

2) PRODUCT TESTING

Get it right. Quality assurance is key. Go together to buy your basic raw ingredients. Return to the factory (your kitchen) and work with your budding entrepreneur to manufacture the product. Find a good recipe. Together make small batches and taste-test.

3) MARKET PRICING

Figure out the cost per cup of the lemonade. This will include the raw ingredients (don't forget the cup) and labor costs. To do this, you'll need to help your child value her time by the hour: an abstract but completely worthwhile lesson on the different components involved in the cost of goods. This should be fun. Knowing the costs will help her to figure out how she will price the lemonade per cup. The difference between the cost of goods and services (her time) and the retail price is her markup. Discuss pricing. If the market doesn't drink at the price she sets, teach her about how markdowns can move a product.

4) STRATEGIC PLANNING

Look at the weather forecast for hot and dry days. Scout busy, safe locations for the stand. Consider whether there is a charity walk planned in your area and help your child set up shop in a safe nearby place. Stay with her.

5) MARKETING

Brainstorm. What would attract interest in her lemonade? How should she represent it? Who would want to buy her product?

Then make posters and ask her to think about where the people who would want lemonade would be likely to see them. Think about posting to a community bulletin board at a local business.

6) PROFIT/LOSS + NEXT STEP

Keep track of how many cups of lemonade are sold and the amount of time she's invested in her venture. (Good record keeping is important in all businesses!) Next, count all of the cash on hand and write down the amount. This is the revenue earned from her effort. Then, multiply the number of cups sold by the cost per cup of the raw ingredients and this will give her the total cost to make all of the lemonade. Subtract this number from the total amount of money collected and the difference is the gross profit. Next subtract the cost of labor and the interest expense from the gross profit to figure out the net profit for her lemonade business.

Easy!

24

INTEGRATING MONEY SENSE
INTO EVERYDAY LIFE

Use real-life opportunities to highlight smart money choices in everyday living. Teach your children to look closely at generics as substitutes for name brands, to help you find and use coupons (remember: *only* for products you would normally buy!), and to be on the lookout for specials, whether it's stocking up on staples like toilet paper or paper towels or indulging in on-sale treats you wouldn't ordinarily splurge on.

Teach them a lifelong habit of recycling and earning, whether on eBay, at the thrift store, or by running a yard sale (see page 57). Invite them to help you in age-appropriate ways, and give them a piece of the action. When they outgrow their trendy clothes (remember those leopard-print fingerless gloves?), go together to the consignment shop.

As they get older, opportunities for earning their own money will increase: car washing, babysitting, lawn mowing, catering, and dog walking are all great choices. But encourage them to think outside the box, too. We know many young entrepreneurs who've used the Internet to sell homemade soaps and fragrances, offer fashion advice, do Web design, sell their music . . . or start a little thing called Facebook.

GOING BEYOND THE BASICS

Once kids have an allowance, it's time to get more invested in teaching them to manage their cash. Open a bank account with them when they are old enough to do simple math and read and write their names.

As they get older and start to earn money on their own, they'll need to set up a checking account and learn how to manage their accounts. They could begin by learning to master an old-fashioned check register, but we don't think it matters all that much. Everything they'll be doing in the future will be online, and they may as well use new, more efficient tools. We do firmly believe that you insist they balance their checking accounts each month. This is nonnegotiable.

Depending on how much money they save from part-time jobs, gifts from relatives, and summer work, you might encourage them to look for higher-interest-paying products—a challenge in this era of low interest. A regular savings account will pay very little. A money market account tied to checking may pay out a bit more. Begin talking with your kids about the stock market and other investment vehicles that help them grow their money.

This conversation can start young. You've been a good mama, having lively dinner table discussions about politics, food, and what happened during the day, while wisely postponing the "why did you get a C-minus in math?" talk. (Right?) Now think about adding finance and money to the menu. When you do this, you add more than financial acumen to their education. You're opening a window into how the world works, even possible career choices.

STOCKS AND BONDS

If you're in the market and own a mutual fund or individual shares in stocks, talk about how the stocks are doing. Track their performance. (A gyrating exercise these days.) If you have a muni bond about to mature, or are making 401(k) or Roth pension investment choices, why not discuss your options?

More tangible, and more likely to ignite their interest, is to talk about consumer products that you and your kids use. Every product you touch, whether it's a picture book you're reading to them, the bike they ride, or their favorite television show, is likely owned by a large publicly traded company.

Make it fun. Make it relevant. Say you have a son who's car crazy and knows all about the new models from General Motors, Ford, Toyota. Look at the product lines, features, pricing. What about Tesla and innovative technologies?

A fashion-conscious kid? Go to J.Crew, the Gap, or Target each season and decide if the clothes are worth buying. Evaluate trends together. Follow their sales to see if you were able to predict whether they would be successful. Help kids get savvy about their passions.

Some companies like Facebook are still private (as of this writing). Amazing. Talk about how entrepreneurs are an engine that drives the economy, about how anyone can take a good idea and, with hard work and luck, make something out of it.

Follow the fortunes of companies your kids believe in, and help them to research the stock. They may even choose to buy a share or two in the company and watch its fortunes rise and fall.

TRADING KIDS

SO YOUR LITTLE one wants to invest in the market. How does she do it?

One method is through a custodial brokerage account. The child's name is on the account, with the parent as a custodian. When the child turns twenty-one (this varies by state), the money is hers. Check with your current broker and see if she can accommodate an account for your child that has a certain amount of "free" trades.

Shop around to find a brokerage house offering a reasonable rate for each stock transaction. Be careful about commissions, monthly charges, and inactivity fees (which can eat up an entire little portfolio). Start by looking at:

TradeKing

OptionsHouse

Zecco

Scottrade

E*TRADE

Beware of the tax traps of such a setup, however, as the first $950 of income is not taxed, the next $950 is at the child's tax rate, and anything above $1,900 is taxed at the parent's tax rate (this is the infamous "kiddie tax" you may have heard about). But if the child's account is small, this shouldn't matter.

REAL ESTATE

We know the days of making a killing on your home are long ago and far away (many of you are *getting* killed instead). Still, talking about how real estate works is smart.

Mortgages are most likely the most significant loan your

kids will assume in their adulthood (and one of the few permitted debt instruments in our book). Talk about yours: how much of it is going toward the principal, how much is going to service the interest payment. It's an eye-opening lesson about how loans work. About why it's important to keep a good credit rating. About how money can be used to make money (in this case, the bank is using your money to make money). Thinking of refinancing, now that interest rates are so low? Talk about it. Help your kids understand how the cost of money fluctuates. So while you're increasing the size of your borrowing, you're paying a similar amount each month because money's less expensive.

We like the other life lessons that real estate can offer. Is your family thinking about moving? Talk about it collectively. Discuss the choices that you have as a family that will influence your decision making: schools, access to services and transportation, services like parks and rec programs, elder care, libraries. See the correlations between pricing and what communities and neighborhoods offer.

A few other lessons can come into play here: insurance and design. Homes that have mortgages must have insurance. It's a great opportunity to discuss how insurance works. You might even use this opportunity to teach them about design (okay, not directly financially related, but it may be career related). Maybe you'll find a young architect, landscape designer, or interior designer sitting at your dinner table whose interest is piqued by Victorian turrets, the Frank Lloyd Wright Prairie School houses, or modern designs in your neighborhood.

TAX TIME

The single biggest shock to young working adults is the bite taxes take out of their paychecks.

"I'm making ten dollars an hour at the town pool! Whoo-hoo! Just ten hours of work and I'll have enough to buy Grand Theft Auto IV!"

Uh, not so fast.

Take time now to educate your kids about how the services around them are funded. Policemen, firefighters, and teachers get paid out of state taxes. Military and postal and TSA workers are paid with federal tax dollars. Explain what Social Security taxes are for and how your children can expect to collect (or not!).

Death and taxes are inevitable. Skip the death part at dinner, but the tax talk (as long as you don't choke) is a good idea.

MONEY MAVEN

Time to take stock. You've cleaned up your own budget. Added to your savings account and begun planning for college and retirement. Improved your sex life (we hope) by facing up to insurance, death, and taxes. You're having grown-up conversations with your kiddos about money and how the real world works. You deserve a bonus. (Or at least a nice glass of wine.)

PART 5

TECHNOMOMS:
Take a Zettabyte Out of Life

INTRODUCTION

Remember the old days, when your parents yelled at you to hang up the phone so they could use it? The TV was a cube. You couldn't pause, rewind, demand shows. You played Tetris on a Game Boy and listened to Michael Jackson on a Walkman. You went to the library to do research. If you needed a ride home from school you used a pay phone. So quaint! Your school applications were completed in pen and ink (remember Wite-Out?) and mailed return receipt requested. Cars did not have GPS systems, so your parents fought about whether to go left or right instead of swearing at some robotic German lady. Kids jabbed one another in the backseat, or played games—counting the number of out-of-state license plates, twenty questions, I spy—and asked repeatedly, "Are we there yet?" (Okay. Some things never change.)

The single computer sat in the family room—a glowing altar. You bought software, downloaded it from a disk. Your parents had no idea what you were doing in AOL chat rooms that you reached through dial-up connections that were slow or busy or cut out midconversation. (Remember that screechy connecting noise, like R2D2 in the throes of wild passion?) And while the mean girls may have teased you, made a few nasty phone calls, passed a note or two, you could go home and find sanctuary.

You get the point.

Nothing is the same. Not for you or for your kids. The entire landscape has twisted and turned and accelerated so fast that keeping up with technology and all things "connected" could drive you over the edge. Not to mention that keeping up with the latest hardware/software could bankrupt you. Most days you feel like there's no way you can get on top of it—forget about keeping on top of your kids who are already on it.

We're going to help you get back in charge.

THE DIGITAL BATTLE

The relentless explosion of products and networks offering *instant access* to nearly everybody and everything is an assault on both your wallet and your parenting skills. The biggest difference today is the intricate connective tissue of the social network. Whether they're texting, gaming, researching, or socializing, chances are your kids are online and communicating with someone who could be anyone—anywhere. This is the ultimate boundary changer. It makes your job—channeling how your kids relate to others, and how they use technology—a generation removed from those AOL chat rooms.

What's a mama to do?

First, you have to get with the program. Then figure out which gizmos and plans your family needs; look for the best value in products and service providers; set the boundaries for where, when, and how your kids use all things wired. Finally, have fun with your kids and embrace the digital age! Yeah, you're a mom, but that doesn't mean you're old and out of touch!

Time to tune in and power up.

25

THE HARD STUFF:
Learn When to Jump
In and How to Buy

DO YOUR HOMEWORK: DON'T BUST YOUR
BUDGET ON THE BLEEDING EDGE

It seems everything you need to be present in the modern world requires an interface, a device, a gadget, a plan. With each new breakthrough, your current products become obsolete.

Before you buy any new piece of electronics for you or the kids, do your homework. We keep up on the latest digital scoop with a few key go-to resources. While others drool over Mr. Six-pack at the gym, we're sweet on David Pogue at the *New York Times* (the tech writer and host of *Making Stuff* on NOVA—a must watch for you and the kiddies). Another brainiac crush? Walter Mossberg of the *Wall Street Journal*, a god of techie decoding. We've also embedded Mashable into our daily information sweep to keep abreast of all things techie and social media. The tech world is constantly changing. If you know where to find good information, it's easier to go with the flow and identify which products and services to plug into.

THE ELECTRONIC WARDROBE

AS A FAMILY, we love to read and write. We watch *Masterpiece*. We go to the ballet. We're also Facebook stalkers. *Fringe* (the TV show) fanatics. Bloggers. Photoshop phenoms. Mad texters. Occasional tweeters. Gamers. Our point? PBS and Super Mario live side by side in the paradoxical high-low life we all lead. You can be a smart, cultured person—*and* raise smart, cultured kids—and be a TV watcher and gamer. The well-stocked modern family will have a combination of one or more of the following:

- desktop computer
- laptop(s) computer/netbook
- HD television
- digital camera/camcorder
- smartphone
- e-book reader
- tablet
- gaming device

DIG (MAYBE, YES, TO CHINA)

Stay abreast of the electronics market by reading our go-to guys, but when it's time to pull the trigger and make a purchase, dig in deeper. Enlist the kids, teach them how to be smart consumers, and have them help you do the research before you buy any new product (techie or otherwise).

The first stop? The buying bible: *Consumer Reports*. Follow up by checking in with *PC Magazine*, CNET, the *Wall Street Journal* tech section, TechCrunch, CrunchGear, *Wired*, ConsumerSearch. Google. Snoop around to find other articles from *reputable* sources. Scroll down the page and read other readers' comments. Look for patterns of satisfaction. Look for common complaints.

From there, head over to the product's home page and look closely at the help line threads (it's smart to do this for most consumables: e-gadget, car, credit card). We were interested in top-of-the-box players to connect streaming Web content like Netflix to our television. One player received wonderful reviews from the critics. The price was right. We were ready to push the "buy" button. But then we noticed that many owners were on the help line because they couldn't get Netflix to load on their boxes. We took a pass. Whew! We saved ourselves dough and time in techie hell.

BETTER THAN A BILLION BLOGS:
One Splurge-worthy Magazine

THE CONSUMER BIBLE is *Consumer Reports*—worth the investment. Buy it. Or at least follow their blogs and go to the library to check out their opinion on any big purchase. A curated take on the good, the bad, and the ugly, the magazine was onto the power of the community to test and evaluate products well before the billion-blog era.

VALUES, BARGAINS, DIRTBALL-CHEAPO PRICING

BE SMART ABOUT buying any items that get lots of use. If you're making a big investment, buy the best you can afford. Factor in warranties and service. You want a product made by a company that offers help without sending you around the world. And don't complicate your life! In the electronics game, plug in and play is the way for us. Unless you've got a whiz kid who can make anything work, keep things simple and streamlined.

Save time. Save aggravation.

TIMING AND TRADING: WHEN TO BUY

When it comes to new gadgets, your kids are like amped-up racehorses at the gate. No slowing them down. You, however, are mature and experienced and patient. (We'll pretend, anyway.) Unlike your kids, you know not to turn into Seabiscuit whenever a new product is announced. You know that to everything there is a season.

Just like apparel retailers bring in new fashions each season (clearing out bikinis to make shelf space for coats), electronics retailers bring in and clear out phones, games, TVs, and computers. Old has to make way for new. And since innovation is their lifeblood, you'll benefit with price reductions in two ways: the cutting-edge way, through advances in technology that reduce product cost (more later), and the old-fashioned way, through moving inventory off shelves to make room for new goods.

When you're in the market for new gear, pay close attention to industry news reports, so you'll know when new products are going to be introduced. This will serve you well as both a buyer and a seller. When a technological leap is in the offing you may decide to wait to purchase: either to take advantage of the new technology or to take advantage of the inevitable price reductions in the existing product line. And as a seller, if an upgraded version of an electronic device is about to hit the market, you'll be able to beat the rush and sell your current—but soon-to-be outdated—product in advance of the introduction. (Providing you can live without your iPad or desktop or old game gear, you'll max out the dollars you receive that can help defray the cost of new gear.)

TURN, TURN, TURN

Since the immutable law of retailing is "out with the old to make room for the new," retailers are always clearing out old stuff to make room for fresh inventory. Major electronics companies unveil many new product lines in January at the Consumer Electronics Show. Do your research, and pay close attention to when new products are timed to hit the stores. Each niche (computer, camera, TV, etc.) in the market has its own particular timing of product delivery. And don't forget retailers are always promoting individual products and categories to drive traffic and business. A savvy consumer will watch sales circulars like a hawk and create alerts on e-sites (see below).

MERRY, MERRY, MERRY

MAKE A CHARGE during the Christmas run-up. Black Friday and the weeks before the holiday will have the big boys using hot electronics as loss leaders to lure you in. Get through it by entering the mom zone (use the measured breathing you learned in labor). Invest the time and effort to brave the throngs.

PATIENCE IS A MONEY-SAVING VIRTUE: CUT OUT BEING FIRST IN LINE

While cutting-edge products are totally sexy and fun, they're pricey and often have some kinks. Kind of like your first boyfriend—exciting, but not really worth the investment. Remember how expensive flat-screen televisions were a few years ago? The original iPhone? Digital cameras? This is an opportunity to teach your kids patience, because they probably *will* be frothing at the mouth to get their hands on the latest and greatest—and the begging and pleading won't be pretty.

So take a pass on that 3-D television no matter how much they are torturing you. Yes, *Toy Story 3* is cute in every dimension, and *Alice in Wonderland* may pop out in all her camp glory, but the TVs are ghastly expensive and the technology has a long way to go. Get the goggles and popcorn at the movie theater. Patience, sister, patience.

FINDING THE RIGHT POSITION: BE SECOND IN LINE

Just like we suggest making a beeline for the clearance rack in the department store and mixing up your clothing purchases with items from consignment, apply the same concept to your electronics purchases. Both stores and individual sellers (remember you're one of them now) offer a robust market in repackaged, refurbished, and used electronics. But hold on! This does not give you a hall pass on doing your homework. A lousy model, whether new, dinged, or bought on eBay, is still a lousy model.

You can save on almost every purchase by first checking in at the clearance centers at stores (brick-and-mortar or online). Often, you'll find brand-new goods with dents and bruises. So what if the Blu-ray DVD player has a scratch on the side or the laptop case is nicked? After it's spent a week in your house do you really think you'll notice?

Other goods you'll find in clearance may have been bought by someone else and taken out of the box for a test run. While not "used," they can't be sold as brand-new. The retailer will have taken it out of the hide of the original buyer with a "restocking" fee, and put the item back out for sale at a reduced price.

The biggest bargains of all will be the refurbished products sold by a reputable store—they should work like new and come with a warranty (read carefully). We once had great luck with a used refurbished Mac laptop, which came with an AppleCare warranty. Snagged at 30 percent markdown. While it wasn't the sleekest of the sleek, it was pretty sexy nonetheless—and it was our workhorse for many years.

THE CLOUD

REMEMBER IN THAT classic movie *The Graduate,* the guy walking around whispering, "Plastic"? Today he might be wandering around whispering, "The cloud." Think of a storage and communication place in the sky where data and information meet in heavenly communion outside the confines of your desktop or personal handheld computing device. No need to ever buy or download a software program. Forget bulky storage solutions. Imagine low-cost computers; imagine traveling anywhere and, as long as you have an Internet connection, having instant access to all your docs, pics, and history.

It's here. Rise and embrace it. (But also keep a thumb drive or hard copy of keepsake pictures and critical information on earth in your own drawer.)

PENNY-PINCHING PINBALL WIZARDS

If you or your kids are gamers, unless you're serious first-edition collectors, *never* pay full price. Major retailers (and the kid down the street) are all selling preowned hardware and games. This doesn't make the industry happy—but we don't feel for them, since soon enough they'll be selling all their games from the cloud and you won't be able to extract the software from your Xbox to trade it.

PAYS TO BE THOROUGH

ALWAYS ASK FOR the warranty or service contract for any used product you're buying. Often this goes with the product, not with the owner. Grab it. If you're comparing computer prices, factor in preloaded programs. Inquire about cables, mice, remotes, and other add-ons. If you're buying from a store, read the fine print with a magnifying glass. Buyer beware: Often store warranties are much shorter on a refurbished product than a new one.

If you see a game, game gear, computer, TV, cell phone, or tablet that you've been hunting for, remember, the used-electronics market is like any commodities market (hey, another educational experience for the wee ones). Prices on secondhand products fluctuate according to demand. Hot items go quickly, so if it's a must-have and a good price—snatch it up.

THE DELL WITH IT

RECENTLY, A FRIEND purchased a brand-new Dell laptop, seduced by a very cheap price and reasonable product reviews. It didn't work right. She spent hours with call centers overseas unable to resolve the problem. As part of the extended service contract she had bought, Dell sent a tech to her house to facilitate the repair. He hadn't bathed in some time; nor had his clothes been washed. (So disturbing was his behavior and appearance, she decided against complaining out of fear the company would fire him and he knew where she lived.) He spent hours on the computer, and, even after all the diagnostic work, it had to go back to Dell for a two-week repair.

(continued)

Her ultimate decision: to cut her losses. She sold the Dell as soon as it came back and converted the cash into a Mac. At least that way, when she has a problem she can walk into the Apple store and speak with a live Genius.

If you have a dog—the hell with it. While there's still value, cash out and convert what you can salvage into a product upgrade.

SMART ONLINE STOPS

FOR PRODUCT COMPARISON pricing and current coupon deals on electronics and other products:

Techbargains.com

Fatwallet.com

Ebates.com

FindersCheapers.com

PriceGrabber.com

PricePlease.com is a site that alerts you to price reductions in products you identify.

SpringPad.com is a very cool general organizer with price-notification features.

CLEAR OUT AND CASH IN

Who doesn't have old cell phones, computers, camcorders gathering dust in the closet? Yes, it's possible that little Ana will grow up and have fond memories of her third digital camera, but not likely. Or are you hanging on to that old Dell because you don't know what else to do with it? More likely.

Below is a list of resources to help you convert the debris into cash (or at least send it on to good green recycling heaven). Compare and contrast pricing, shipping charges, and how they pay you. As in all online transactions, be wary. Get paid up front or have a transaction happen via a secure method like PayPal.

Click Here to Trade It In. . . .

Gazelle.com

EcoSquid.com

YouRenew.com

BuyMyTronics.com

Instantsale.ebay.com

BestBuy.com

(These sites will also give you a baseline sense of market pricing for used products you may be thinking of buying.)

Click Here to Give It Away. . . .

Know about the Freecycle Network (www.freecycle.org)?

Great for more than just giving an old gadget a second life, this is a "grassroots and entirely nonprofit movement of people who are giving (and getting) stuff for free in their own towns. It's all about reuse and keeping good stuff out of landfills." Check for a group in your community.

IT PAYS TO BE NEUROTIC

- Buying from an individual seller may offer the best deal, but buy pricey products only if they come with a verifiable warranty or service contract. That big-screen TV or laptop or iPad is no bargain if the screen goes blank a week after you buy it—the guy who lives at Third and Elm does not process returns.

- If you are buying a used item in person from a private seller, be wary of where you meet him (or her) with a wad of cash in hand.

- *Hot electronics* listed on Craigslist and eBay may be just that: hot.

- When selling, remember to "clear" your items of personal information. Don't trust resellers or anyone else who says they'll do it for you. Do it yourself. Remember to take memory cards out of cameras and keep them. Do you really want Joe Schmo having access to those pictures of the birth you forgot to delete? (Your screaming expression at eight centimeters isn't exactly something you want made public.)

ERASE YOURSELF

FROM MICROSOFT ON how to clear a PC:
  http://www.microsoft.com/athome/organization/personal files.aspx
FROM CNET about clearing out your Mac: http://download.cnet .com/CleanMyMac/3000-2094_4-10904833.html
FROM APPLE on how to zero out all information on a disk:
  http://support.apple.com/kb/HT1820
(By the way: Using a magnet as a way to erase memory is an urban legend.)

THUMBS-UP TO E-HAND-ME-DOWNS

While we have a soft spot for kids wanting to express their own identity in their clothing choices, there's nothing more obnoxious than a little whippersnapper in fifth grade all pimped out in gleaming new e-hardware.

Trade up, treat yourself, and hand down your old gizmos to the munchkins.

JUST LIKE EVE

WE'VE BITTEN THE Apple and we're hooked. Not that we haven't found a few worms on the way. For a stylish mama, few tech objects are as crisp and elegant. For a tech-challenged mama, few companies can tempt you with better service. We're still running the original iPhone and have never had a moment of trouble—it's even still "going" on the original battery. (Proving cheapest is not always the best value.) Our MacBook Air, hmm, we've had a few glitches, but credit Apple with replacing a troubled machine, after two full years of use, with a brand-new, fully loaded beauty.

26

MONOPOLY, ANYONE?
Play the Media Game—and Save

Few tasks can get a woman moaning so fast as figuring out which telecommunications/cable gadget, gizmo, or plan is the right one for her family. No, we're not talking *good* moaning— we're talking root-canal-without-benefit-of-numbing-agent moaning. Who knew anything could make you yearn for the no-choice Ma Bell era? And we suspect you share our nostalgia and our pain.

Even though you may hate the cable guy—and have fantasies of transforming into the mom from *Terminator* and disabling the entire cellular network—the work involved in getting out of these relationships is exhausting. We know it's easier to stay in a dysfunctional relationship than make a change. (Ring a bell?) Just know if the relationship is abusive, you do have options.

THE CONNECTION

While there are many options to circumnavigate cable and dish, unless you're a geek, or geek-connected, it's still the simplest way to get both the plumbing and the content juice into your house. In most areas you'll find competition. With the telephone companies moving in on the cable guys, and the dish guys trying to lure you, shop around and see where you get the best price, then play them off one another.

Bundling Internet, cable television, and phone services can offer price savings. But after the introductory special, bundled pricing tends to rise . . . so take this into account when you're shopping. Ask whether the provider will guarantee the special price for the entire contract. Find out about early termination fees. As in all things, negotiate.

**BUNGLED BUNDLE BILLS
BURGLE BUDGETS
(Say That Fast Ten Times in a Row!)**

DON'T GET RIPPED off! Make sure you read and understand each line item of your monthly charges. Unscrupulous companies have been known to routinely add unauthorized charges to bills.

Check back every six months (put this on your calendar! Really!) to make sure you're getting the best current pricing. We recently saved $40/month simply because we called and asked if ours was the best available rate.

SHOULD YOU CUT THE CORDS?

The telephone and cable television cords, that is.

Since you're a normal mom, we're certain the threat to cut the cable cord and toss the television has passed your lips more than once. We're with you on this. The mind-numbing passivity your kids exhibit while watching the dumber-than-dumb drivel is enough to make a smart mom homicidal. Still, we know killing the TV is an idle threat. (Besides, there's no reason you should deprive yourself of *The Killing, Game of Thrones*, or *Mad Men*.) Your kids know it, too. So let's get real.

First, set rules and boundaries about what they watch, when they watch, and how long they watch—and stick to them. This is called good parenting. It's work. It takes resolve and it's what kids need. Boundaries. As for dumping cable or satellite to reduce your expenses, this can work, too.

WHAT'S A HOT SPOT, AND IS IT G-RATED?

VERY SIMPLY PUT, a "hot spot" is a place you can catch a wi-fi signal to connect to the Internet. In your house you've got a router that broadcasts the hardwired signal from your Internet service provider. When you're on the go, there are public signals you pick up or pay to connect to. These days, you can even turn your own smartphone (or other devices) into a mobile hot spot, so you're connected wherever you go. Yes, this is the brave new world, and it's where your kids are living.

If you use your smartphone as a hot spot (and "tether" other devices to it—computers, tablets, etc.), make sure you know how this affects your data usage charges. (See info about data on page 215; see info about security on page 225.)

Before you haul out the scissors, though, remember the easiest first step to saving is to cut back on your current service package. Quit the premium channels. Get all the pricey converter boxes out of all the rooms; save the family room or your bedroom (moms need to take care of themselves). By the way, your kids don't have televisions in their rooms. Right? Yes, we *are* judging. So you won't be paying for a box for them. Right?

TURN IT ON ONLY WHEN YOU NEED TO
(We Know You're Good at This.)

SOME CABLE CONTRACTS will allow you to turn service on and off without penalty. So, just like your favorite shows go on summer break, consider sending the television on an occasional hiatus. We have friends who enhance their cable package during the summertime (big baseball fans). When autumn comes, it's back to PBS and public access.

BIG LOVE

Once you're covered on basic television needs for local news, network programs, etc., you can cut the cord by partnering with other devices and services to bring programming, Web, and multimedia content directly into your life. (And you thought polygamy just benefited guys?)

Top-of-set boxes and game stations offer a conduit for you to bring free and for-pay Internet Web programming to your television set. Once you invest in one of these, you might kill cable/dish altogether, or just use these as an add-on to the basic cable.

Or, for the greatest savings and most control over what your kids watch, you may decide to use computers and laptops to satisfy your entertainment needs. Learn to hook the computer to an HDTV with your own hardware cable. (Note: Resolution may be compromised. But the savings may help you see more clearly.)

TOP OF BOX—TOP OF WORLD?

IT'S WELL WORTH looking into what top-of-set boxes like Boxee Box, PlayOn, Roku, Apple TV, and Google can offer. Even game stations can be used as a conduit to stream programming to your television. Each has a slightly different interface and offers access to different content.

Not only will they bring in for-pay entertainment, like Netflix or Hulu Plus, but they'll seamlessly stream a mind-boggling array of other content, original and vintage, from highbrow university lectures to original *Daria* episodes—most for free.

(No wonder Comcast bought NBC, and Netflix is producing its own content—with these alternative ways to stream content to your sets, it's very possible you'll just be using the cable guys to do the plumbing.)

BE CONTENT WITH ALTERNATE PLUG-INS

Whether or not you buy a box, you'll find endless free media available to watch on your computer. Just like authors are bypassing traditional publishers to bring books to market, so too are video content producers bypassing the traditional distribution arms to bring original programming to the Web. (Find a list of free channels on our Web site.)

27

THE PHONE DECODER:
How Did
"Bringg, Bringgg, Bringgg"
Become
"Like Baby, Baby, Baby, Oh!"

Life used to be simpler.
You had a landline and maybe a fax. You had a cell phone and it was for talking. Now you wonder, do you even need a landline? And is the cell a phone for chatting or is it a computer or a video player or a debit card? Your telecommunications expenses are growing exponentially. It's smart to take a step back. Examine what devices you're using, how they can be most cost-effective, and how your kids plug into the data stream.

BY LAND: DOES ANYONE REALLY USE A TELEPHONE ANYMORE?

According to the cell phone industry trade group CTIA, in 2010 almost a quarter of all households in the United States had junked their landlines. Assuming you haven't already tossed

211

yours in the trash pile, ask yourself: Can you save money *now* by eliminating your landline?

THE LANDLINE DIAGNOSTIC

- Do you live in an area where cell service is spotty?
- Do you have a home security system that at present connects only through a landline?
- Do you worry a cell phone will fail you in the event of an emergency?
- Do you worry that emergency responders will not be able to find you (the location of 911 calls made on landlines are visible at the dispatch station)?
- Do you need telephone service if the power goes down?

If you answered yes to any of these questions, you need a landline (for now).

Now step back and look at the entire picture. Determine how this phone will be used and pick a plan accordingly. Will it be for emergency backup? Or will it be your workhorse phone connection for the kids to talk to Grandma in Florida and to make sleepover plans?

GET A PHONE REDUCTION

STILL PAYING FOR phone enhancements like call waiting, call messaging, call forwarding? Be honest, with digital readouts showing who called, do you even listen to your messages? Do you need these services? If someone urgently needs to find you, they'll text or e-mail. Cancel if you're paying extra.

MIX AND MATCH

If you decide to cut the cord or augment a basic hardwired service, you have two broad options: cell service and VoIP (Voice over Internet Protocol service). If you're currently getting home phone service from your cable provider, you're using VoIP. You also have options beyond your cable provider. Start by looking at Vonage, Ooma, and magicJack. As of this writing, no-cost VoIP options like Skype and Google are not as convenient to use and are unlikely to be a practical only-phone connection for your family, although they are a bargain choice for overseas calls.

Whatever direction you take, check in periodically with the provider(s) to make sure you're getting the best price. (Think about it: When was the last time someone called joyously offering a price reduction?)

BY AIR: TALK FIRST

Which cell plan makes sense for the family? Sit down together and discuss everything from texts to talk to data time. Work out a reasonable plan together. If you just hand a kid a phone and he hasn't participated in this discussion, he won't have ownership. Know that you can easily monitor his usage online. Almost all new phones will have built-in data and talk-minutes usage monitors, so there's no excuse for a big uh-oh at the end of a month. According to the Pew Research Center: "Unlimited plans are tied to increases in use of the phone, while teens on 'metered' plans are much more circumspect in their use of the phone."

TEXTZILLA NATION

- According to CTIA, in 2005 we sent 81 billion texts. In 2010, that number blew past 2.1 *trillion*. (Like we need to tell you— you have kids.)

- According to the Pew Research Center, one in three teens sends more than three thousand text messages a month. That's more than a hundred daily.

CELL PHONES AND PIERCINGS: WHEN?

Ask anyone what's the appropriate age for a child to have their ears (or other body parts) pierced or to get their own cell phone and you'll need to put earplugs in. Everyone will have a different opinion. The right answer?

It's up to you. Only one thing is certain: You can't avoid the "to cell phone or not to cell phone" discussion. A recent survey by the Yankee Group reported that by 2013 half of kids ages eight to twelve will have cell phones.

Wrap your head around this: Most tweens and teens are not chattering away; they're texting. So if every eight- or nine-year-old in your school district has a cell phone and your kid doesn't, how will he communicate? Will it make him a social outcast?

Start with a prepaid cell plan. This is a safe (for the wallet) and time-contained way to ease kids into the responsibility of having a phone. If they have only x number of texts or minutes per month, they'll learn to budget pretty quickly.

Remember, a cell phone for a youngster is a privilege, not a right, and as with all privileges it needs to be earned and not abused. In fact, it's a good idea for kids to contribute a portion of the phone's cost and upkeep (data plan) through money earned babysitting, lawn mowing, helping tech-challenged adults use new technology. And even though we're not punitive by nature, the loss of cell privileges is a really good threat to hang over them.

The piercing part, well . . . there are worse things than pierced ears—right?

THE DEVIL'S IN THE DATA

Your kids will be doing more than texting. Just like you, they'll be using the Internet for Facebook, Twitter, and apps, to play games, take and send pictures, watch video and movies. All this requires transmitting data on the information superhighway, and the cell companies are starting to charge you big-time. What used to be critical when buying a cell plan was voice minutes and service coverage; now it's equally important to select and manage the best text and data plan for you and your family. This is starting to get very pricey. Streaming video, music and apps are big data hogs, so drum into your kiddos' heads that they must connect with a WiFi signal whenever they are using their smartphones.

As your family's gadget collection grows, don't forget to factor into your expenses the data usage fees for your other wired/wireless devices (like tablets, readers, and computers). We just finished looking at the à la carte pricing menu on the AT&T site and we're reaching for our evening cocktail. And it's only ten in the morning.

A LONG LIST OF SMART THINGS TO ASK
BEFORE YOU BUY A NEW PHONE OR PLAN

- Can you take the phones out for a test drive before signup? You need to make sure your house and daily route are not sitting in the middle of that carrier's dead zone.

- Is there an activation fee? Will they waive it if you sign on the dotted line?

- Is there a termination fee for ending the contract? Will they waive it if you sign up today?

- If one phone is lost or stolen and has to be replaced on a family plan, does it by default extend the entire contract beyond the original length? (And what happens if the replacement phone is not purchased through the carrier?)

- Data minutes: How are they computed? Is there an easy way to keep on top of them?

- Texts? How many? How do you monitor them?

- Are there filtering devices and other parental controls that can be applied to kids' phones? What is the fee?

- Do unused minutes or data roll over to the next month?

- What are their coverage areas? Are there roaming fees if you're outside the coverage area? If they say it is "national" service, does this mean just within their network or for all calls? Who falls into the "friends and family" network?

- Will the phone alert you when you are about to incur roaming charges?

- Will the phone alert you when you are about to go over minutes or data usage?

- Who pays for incoming calls if they are from a carrier outside your network?

WHAT'S THE RISK?

THE INSURANCE QUESTION is a toughie.

If you're constantly losing things—or your kids are—then it's a good idea to insure a cell phone. But think about it—after two years of paying several bucks a month, you may end up paying double what the phone cost.

We choose to live dangerously and have never insured our phones.

LOCAL BARGAINS

Don't forget that local cell carriers can offer big savings: C Spire, Cricket, Metro PCS, U.S. Cellular, and Virgin Mobile all offer cheap plans (although, except for C Spire, sadly, no iPhones). When you're in the hunt, compare and contrast benefits with the big national carriers: AT&T, Verizon, Sprint, and T-Mobile.

DON'T GET SCREWED WHILE TRAVELING

If you travel overseas, call your carrier before you leave and check into their plans. We've found pricing ghastly and instead purchase a disposable cell in foreign countries. Unless you've worked out an overseas package with your carrier, do not, we repeat, *do not* power up to check your e-mail or texts; the data cost is prohibitive. If you want to play games or read something already downloaded on your phone, make certain you remain in airline mode. If you're traveling with your kiddies, confiscate their phones and save everyone the aggravation of a big surprise when you get home to your cell bills. You know your Juliet won't be able to refrain from making "one quick call" to Romeo back in the States. So take her phone away and let her lament her star-crossed young love.

EVERYTHING IS A NEGOTIATION

OUR ONE FIRM word of advice? Take a page from your kid's playbook—always negotiate. Most of these carriers want to keep you on or sign you up. Face it, if you leave (even if they suck the life out of you by penalizing you for breaking the contract) they've lost a steady revenue stream. And if they don't sign you up they'll never have the chance to suck you dry.

Bargain for cell services. Bargain for Internet services. Bargain for bundled cable, Internet, phone services.

A smart mama is a tough negotiator.

BRAINS + CELL PHONES + EARPIECES

YOU'VE HEARD THE buzz about cell phones and radiation and cancer, but have you been listening?

You vaguely remember the studies warning of this link. But then there were the other studies saying the cell/cancer link is inconclusive, letting you off the hook, so you and the kids haven't consistently used earphones. Trust us, we know it's a pain in the a** to plug in an earbud or headset. You lose them. They're uncomfortable. They break.

Well, it's time to reinvest in earphones for your entire cell phone chatting cohort.

The Journal of the American Medical Association recently published a study showing that a "50-minute cell phone exposure was associated with increased brain glucose metabolism in the region closest to the antennae." That's enough to put us on high alert and not wait for proof-positive evidence that cell phones can do nasty things.

No need to get hysterical and forsake all cells; instead head out the door for new earbuds and make your kids vow to use them. By the way, mama, this is a "splurge-worthy" item. Poor-quality buds will have your tween blasting her music, and evidence is mounting that loud plug-ins are causing hearing loss. (Nothing is easy. Sorry.)

I SPY FOR THE KPC GENERATION

We're not in favor of furtive spying on anyone, particularly the ones we love. Since open lines of communication are the key to mutual respect, discuss all aspects of phone safety with kids before they have a cell phone.

Remember, they're kids. They're learning, and don't yet have all the tools to make good judgments. They will make mistakes.

If you choose to install monitoring devices, be clear with your kids about when/how you'll be monitoring their cell use.

For cell safety, check in with your provider to find out about monitoring add-ons to your basic service. Consider these two programs that allow you to more closely supervise their activities: MyMobileWatchdog.com and KidPhoneAdvocate.com.

Oh, and KPC? Know what that means? They do. "Keeping parents clueless."

Learn the "Top 50 Internet Acronyms Parents Need to Know" at www.netlingo.com/top50/acronyms-for-parents.php.

THROUGH THE GENERATIONS

DROIDS, IOS, POP3, hyperlink, hypertext, applet, bitstream, megapixel, Flash. You listen, nod your head, perhaps even echo the words, not entirely certain you're using them properly—but, hey, no one corrects you. So when ads on television and bill-boards sprang up touting the 3G and the 4G network, you were sure it was some new giga-tera-bit-byte thing that only those on the cutting edge got. Well, we'll admit we only recently realized all this "G" stuff stands for is the next generation of the technology that drives the data network. Each new generation means data will stream faster and smoother—but don't go buying a 4G phone just because it's 4G yet. There are lots of "standards" for 4G, and as of this writing the networks aren't all fully finished (and each carrier is built to different specs). Not all those who currently own these enhanced phones can even drive them at full speed because the roads aren't fully built. Patience, mama, patience.

28

BOUNDARY CHANGER:
The Internet, Social Media, and the Transformation of the Entire Universe

The digital age is the consummate paradox. It's connected and disconnected us. It's freed up time, only to waste it. It's made Beijing present and your partner invisible. (They're on the couch next to you.) It's brought G- and X-rated addictions into your life. It's found you old friends. It's found you new friends. It's lost you other friends (remember that e-mail sent in the heat of the moment?). It's improved your writing skills and limited your speaking skills. It's brought you instant gratification and been the source of infinite information.

It saves you money. It costs you money. Maybe it's even made you money.

Blogger. Photographer. Videographer. Think something, imagine anything, write it, draw it, sing it, film it, and blast it into the world in permanent digital ink. Share news, complaints, creations with next-door neighbors, chums in Chile, strangers in the universe.

Not to get all metaphysical or anything, but it's blurred the boundaries of time and space and reality.

So, is this a good thing?

Yes and no. (Remember, we're talking paradox here.) And to tell you the truth, it doesn't really matter, because there's no plugging this genie back into the bottle. It has changed our lives. And, since you're the mom, it's your job to get with the program.

ARE YOU A SUCCESSFUL MULTITASKING MOM?

Do you switch seamlessly between texting, e-mailing, and surfing the Web while watching television, running laundry, loading dishes, offering homework assistance, and catching up with your best friend on the phone?

Do you keep up a running dialogue with your sister in Sacramento, your colleagues in Colorado, or the credit officer at your bank while you drop off and pick up the kids, the dog, the cleaning?

Once the car is in park, do you whip out a smartphone, check e-mail, Facebook, Twitter, brush your hair, check your teeth, touch up your lipstick all in one fluid motion? (Wait. Worse yet, are you one of those people who do this and stay in the car while a line builds waiting for your parking space?)

While working, do you click between Excel, Word, Scrabble (with random strangers), Style Watch, your Facebook wall, Twitter, CNN, your three e-mail accounts, and randomly Google your old boyfriend, the mother down the street with the seemingly perfect life, summer camp programs for your kids, and the WebMD Symptom Checker?

You're not alone, and of course it's not all bad. But have you considered what you're teaching the little monsters? We'll wager that if you responded yes to any of our scenarios, your car rides feature each member of the family texting, watching a screen, and plugged into a headset. Dinner may convene around the television and is interrupted by a chorus of dings and dongs. In the evening everyone retires to their own corners with their own devices to continue connecting in virtual arenas.

It's time to download some updates.

END THE MULTITASKING ELECTRONIC ADDICTION

We know it's hard. There are no boundaries anymore, no peace. The ding alerting you to a text, the beep signaling an e-mail, the tweet announcing a, well, tweet—it could be a kid in need, your boss with a crisis, or confirmation of Saturday-night plans. Time to shut it off—at least some of the time. Wait until the kids are grown and gone and then you're free to leave the real for the virtual world. Think of this as the same kind of modeling you exhibit by not downing cocktails nightly, smoking, and having wild parties. Control your digital drive. This is the first step.

Then you need to set rules for the kiddies.

Think that multitasking is getting them ready for the real world? Think again. Studies show that different parts of the brain are activated when they multitask, as opposed to when they focus on one task. Ultimately, they may be compromising their ability to apply learned information in abstract ways.

Okay. If we still don't have your attention, shut the damn computer down and listen to this. A recent Kaiser Family Foundation study reported that kids ages eight to eighteen today spend an average of (sit down) seven hours and thirty-eight minutes a day using entertainment media. If you factor in their multitasking (listening to music while tweeting, while on the computer), the number goes up to *eleven* hours a day.

Think about this: Studies show that the more education your

kids get, the more money they'll earn later in life. Constant multitasking whittles down their attention spans; it's antithetical to rigorous, sustained learning. We believe that curbing the family's electronic/plugged-in time helps give kids a real chance to thrive academically. Not to sound superalarmist or anything, but you don't want your kiddos to be dependent on you *forever*, do you?

Be smart. Set the rules and pull the plug. Think about starting with no television, no Internet, no texting, no telephone talking (well, that part seems easy, since talking on the phone is a vestige of another era anyway) until all homework is complete. Set clear limits; for instance, no Facebook during the school week. Nonschool-related computer time for one hour. No television/computer watching during the school week, or limit it to one hour a night. All electronic gear off by nine p.m.

Clearly, if kids are spending so much time plugged in, those hours are getting taken from another activity—most likely sleep. Sleep is critical to good academic performance. Sleep is critical to good decision making. Work hard at getting their lives back in balance, so that they can get the rest they need (and someday move out of the house—so you can get the rest *you* need).

SILENCE IS GOLDEN

IMAGINE A TIME each day when no one talks to you.

Not a sound in the house.

No lights. No camera. No action.

No artificial stimulation. (Hmm.)

Some experts believe that a little loneliness is a good thing, allowing a way to check in with yourself.

For tweens and teens in the process of figuring out who they are, it's not a bad idea to work in a little bit of peaceful, nonpunitive, timed time-out every day.

Om.

CYBERWORRY: SAFETY ONLINE IS JOB #1

From social networking to credit-card information to bill paying to enabled cookies, the digital revolution has opened an insecure portal into your family's safety and bank accounts. These are some basic rules you and your kids should follow.

NEVER DIVULGE YOUR REAL NAME/LOCATION IN AN OPEN SOCIAL NETWORK

This is a major challenge, as many social networking sites are enhancing the user experience with check-in locations. While this is to make it fun to locate and meet up with friends, it's also to enhance/sell e-commerce opportunities.

ALWAYS LOG OFF LINE

Whether at a public terminal or a friend's house or a hotel, teach your kids to log out when they are finished.

KEEP PASSWORDS PRIVATE

While Clyde is Connor's best friend and blood brother today, Mortal Kombat may be in store tomorrow. Teach your kids not to share their password with anyone, ever. Insist that passwords be at least six characters and include a mix of lower- and upper-case letters, numbers, and symbols.

LEARN TO IDENTIFY SPAM AND PHISHING E-MAIL

- Major companies do not send e-mail through public sites such as Gmail, Hotmail, or MSN. Don't open anything, even if it's from a business you are a customer of, if the address contains one of those (e.g., accounts/yourbank@ msn.com). A typical legitimate address will be something like customerservice@yourbank.com—a unique domain name, no odd periods or dashes in the company name.

- Reputable companies will directly address you in an
  e-mail, will never, ever ask for any personal information,
  will not threaten you or create false urgency in their
  message, and will not send you an attachment to open.
  If you receive something from a bank or security account,
  do not respond via e-mail. Call your bank. If you receive
  something from Amazon or eBay or Apple, go to their
  Web site and make contact with them from a reliable
  address. Pass this message on to your kids.

NEVER OPEN E-MAIL FROM UNKNOWN SOURCES
Period.

MORE THAN A MAMA

IF NOT NOW, then soon, you'll be caught in the squeeze of helping out aging parents and relatives as you are raising your own
little ones. Internet and phone scams target the elderly. Share
these rules with the older folks in your family. If you're not raised
from birth in the virtual world, you're at particular risk (like we
need to tell you).

DO NOT OPEN FILES IN MASS E-MAILS
Even if the source seems familiar, like Twitter or Facebook. Major companies do not send e-mail attachments. And while we
hope you're raising sweet and compassionate children, *never, ever*
respond to any solicitations online for money. Period.

NEVER DIVULGE THE FOLLOWING INFORMATION IN AN ONLINE REQUEST

- Social Security number
- mother's maiden name
- credit-card number

DELETE KNOWN JUNK/SPAM

Do not open it. Do not hit "unsubscribe." This just lets the spammers on the other end know they hit a live address. The crap will increase exponentially.

NO DOWNLOADING ANY PROGRAMS, GAMES, OR CONTENT WITHOUT YOUR PERMISSION

Save your computer from spyware, malware, crashing.

POSTER CHILDREN

POST A LIST of the computer rules above the family computer or on the fridge. Make this public. Point it out. Update regularly. Then they can't claim, "I didn't know!" when they borrow your credit card to purchase a Burmese python. Transparency is key.

TEACH YOUR CHILDREN

Kids are using public wi-fi all the time, so help them do it safely. Make sure they know that in a public space your wireless device can be hacked. Some tips:

- Always use a firewall.
- Check the network's privacy statement about encryption—if there's no statement, don't use the network.

- No typing credit-card numbers or passwords.

- Turn off the network when not using it.

- Use common sense—make sure there's no one peeping over your shoulder.

THE SOCIAL NETWORK

Facebook is *the* connecting tissue of the social network. Officially, you must be at least thirteen to open a Facebook account. (This is also the "official" age to open a Twitter account.) While we don't always believe in following the rules, trust us on this one: Obey this rule. Do not aid or abet your children in opening these accounts. If they already have them, ask them to close them. (Yeah, we know, easier said than done.) As for the Facebook-look-alike networks built for younger kids—skip them. The longer the kids wait to enter this world, the longer you'll have one less worry on your doorstep.

Once they're old enough to participate in open online social forums, make sure the privacy settings allow only friends and family access to their profile. Teach your kids to not "publicize" their feelings. Child predators hunt kids who seem vulnerable. Drill into them that they are *never, ever* to talk with any stranger they have met online. If anyone they don't know wants to see them, they are to come to you *immediately*.

This is, first and foremost, about their safety. But it's also about your family's financial security. You don't want the expense of dealing with compromised bank accounts or private data or a screwed-up computer. Once your kids are old enough to be navigating the online world, they're old enough to understand identity and monetary theft—and to know about the sadly huge array of predators out there. Better to educate them about the big, bad world than to keep them sheltered and vulnerable.

RIGHT ON TIME: CIRCUIT BREAKERS

- **SelfControl.com** (http://visitsteve.com/made/selfcontrol/)
  Allows you to lock down specific Web sites for a period of time—Mac only.
- **Freedom.com** (http://www.macfreedom.com/)
  Cuts the cord on all Internet access for up to eight hours—Mac and PC.
- **LeechBlock.com** (https://addons.mozilla.org/en-US/firefox/addon/leechblock/)
  Works on the Firefox browser, allowing you to block sites completely or for scheduled periods (say, six p.m. to nine p.m. study time). Allows you to track time on specific sites.

OVERSIGHT

Ideally, you and your kids will have an open dialogue about limits and dangers online. But they're kids, and their judgment isn't always the best. So here are a few low-cost, low-test ways to keep a gentle eye on them:

- Keep the computer in the family room as long as you can. There is nothing wrong with the over-the-shoulder peek. Walking into a room and seeing the mouse move and the screen flip as you enter is a good tip your kid has been somewhere he shouldn't have been.

- Check in to see where they have been traveling. Be suspicious if there is no history. (We all have history, right?) Someone who has erased it doesn't want you to know where he or she has been.

- Set up boundaries on the computer so kids can't get into trouble by taking a detour into the wrong neighborhood. If you have a PC with a Microsoft OS or an Apple, explore the parental blocks they offer. If you use a PC go to Norton Online Family at https://onlinefamily.norton.com/familysafety/loginStart.fs. The base service is free and the program gets rave reviews. What we like about this as a starter program is that it emphasizes communication.

- As kids get older, or if you have a five-year-old computer savant, you'll need more sophisticated and more expensive programs. For a comprehensive roundup of your choices check online at *PC Magazine*.

SHOP SECURE

SHOP ONLY AT Web sites that have URL bars that read https:// companyname.com with a yellow lock icon or green address bar. You should be able to click on the lock icon and read the site's security certificate.

WRITING IN PERMANENT DIGITAL INK IS COSTLY

Bullies are not new. What *is* new is a nasty note, a vicious rumor, a revealing photograph that doesn't go away, that spreads and replicates. Kids today find no sanctuary and no margin for error. Educate yourself about kids and cyberbullying. Try to reinforce the dangers of writing, posting, and sexting (a costly criminal offense that can ruin lives—theirs and their friends). Here is a list of helpful resources:

- ConnectSafely: http://connectsafely.org
- Stop Bullying: http://www.stopbullying.gov
- National Crime Prevention Council: http://www.ncpc.org/cyberbullying
- Cyberbullying Research Center: http://www.cyberbullying.us/
- It Gets Better Project: http://www.itgetsbetter.org/
- National Network to End Domestic Violence Technology Safety: http://www.nnedv.org/resources/safetynetdocs.html

WHOM DO YOU TRUST?

For every budget-conscious consumer, access to free information is a boon. For every budget-conscious consumer, access to free information is a snake pit. Sorting out fact from fiction and hustle from information is the biggest challenge of the digital age.

Beyond the obvious worry of porn, predators, and scams, you should be worried about the credibility of everything you read and see. From the Photoshopping of supermodels to kids' channels setting up interactive sites promoting their brand and advertising products, to politicians offering you a bridge to nowhere, to content farms churning out fatuous content to drive their sites to the top of Google search, you need to question everything you find on the Internet. And you need to teach your children to question everything they find on the Internet.

ADVERGAMES

Marketers trying to influence little Alice to influence you to buy products like Honeycomb cereal or a Happy Meal or Hasbro's

Littlest Pet Shop have found a haven on the Internet. While children's television commercial time is strictly regulated, no such constraints bind these brands online. To hustle their products they've created interactive sites that appear to children like games and fun contests. So take the mouse, click around, and show your kids how these sites are just big fat commercials. Better yet, find better things for the kids to do.

SHOW AND TELL

Mouse around at home to give your kids concrete examples of product placements and tricky sites. Teach them about cookies (no, not the chocolate-chip variety) and how crafty marketers use them to monitor their Internet usage and target them directly. Teach them about reliable sources. Take them by the hand and go to your local public library. Yes, that building in the real world. You know the one with the door, the roof, the sign that says, LIBRARY? Yep, they still exist. Go there. Ask if a librarian or media specialist can sit down with you and your child and talk about credible sources: about scholarly research with citations, edited news sources, and the difference between opinion pieces and fact pieces, between real journalism and blogger news. Teach them to separate "I feel" from "I think" and "I know" from "I believe."

Check out the Web site of Harvard University's Berkman Center for Internet and Society. You'll find lots of wonderful writing about cyberspace, its benefits, its dangers, its complexities. Their "Youth and Media" project investigates the ramifications of growing up in this deeply connected, virtual world.

OUR HOUSE OF WORSHIP:
The Public Library

IN THE DIGITAL age it's all too easy for kids to miss out on the pleasure and majesty of the public library. (We read with horror about the closing of some and the turning into digital automats of others.)

You'll find real books (remember them?) and DVDs, digital portholes to connect through, lectures and book readings. They even have e-books to borrow, which you can download to your e-reader from the comfort of your couch.

Go to the library and experience a sense of calm that is fast becoming a vestige of another era. Instill in your kids a life-long love of books and a reverence for quiet, unplugged contemplation.

29

YOU'VE GOT THE GOODS—
Now Use Them

We've told you how to go about purchasing the stuff; we've saved you dough; we've warned you about the dangers. Now it's time to put the stuff to good use and have some fun.

MY TURN!

What about *you*? A mom needs to harness this brave new world, just like her kids do. Don't deny yourself pleasure and growth.

News flash: There *is* intelligent life in the universe, and there are plenty of supportive moms out there to connect with. Pose questions about the new video game your son is insistent on buying to a huge community of moms who have firsthand knowledge. Or find out where to stay near Gettysburg when you take the kids on the Civil War tour. We believe in the power of the mom community to make you feel less alone doing what is the toughest job we know. Just make sure you stay connected live in person with real folks, too.

MAMA KNOWS BEST:
Go-to Mama Resources

CafeMom
Mamapedia
MothersClick
Chookooloonks
Bug and the Sweet Banana
MomsLikeMe
MomsRising
BlogHer
Rookie Moms
Smart Mama, Smart Money
BabyCenter
Dooce
Babble
I Am Lotus, aka Sarcastic Mom
Scary Mommy
The *New York Times* Motherlode blog
Free-range Kids
The Pioneer Woman
The Hipster Mom
The Stir by CafeMom

E-BOOKS AND TABLETS

Life is one big paradox, right? Case in point: We love ballet *and* we ogle Lady Gaga. We get pleasure and peace at the public library *and* we're complete converts to the pleasure and ease of a Kindle, Nook, or iPad.

While borrowing books is cost-effective, and reading from a real book is a genuine experience, e-readers are awesome, too. Many books in the public domain are easily downloaded for free.

Think of the classics on every school reading list: *Moby-Dick* and *Pride and Prejudice*. Libraries also have e-books for electronic loan—remember, you don't even have to leave your couch to borrow them.

Think beyond the book. Magazines and newspapers are still developing models for distributing their content through this channel. While it's not sorted out completely, it's likely that if you're a home subscriber, soon you'll be able to download the same magazine or newspapers. Imagine being on the train and reading the *Tribune*, "paging" through *Real Simple* for a good dinner recipe, and catching up on the latest *New Yorker* piece, all on a simple-to-hold, easy-to-carry reader. (Lovely thought, right? Being on the train alone and having the time to read!)

Think about the endless possibilities of reading in an expanded dimension. Connect instantly to sites that take you further in depth or to a related video or piece of music. If you're a mom of a child whose learning style is visual or aural, imagine all the ways he or she can connect with information and ideas. Each device has different features, and you'll need to evaluate which suits your lifestyle and needs. Unless you find yourself on the road and out of reach of reliable wi-fi networks, skip the 3G data up-charge.

WE TAKE IT BACK, AL—WE REALLY LOVE YOU

HOW FITTING THAT *Our Choice* by Al Gore was the first full-length interactive book. Published by Pushcart Press last year, it unleashes the wonder of using a connected digital platform as a reading and learning tool. The coolest feature? A windmill graphic that demonstrates how wind disperses by the reader blowing (yes, we said blowing) on the screen. Watch at www .ted.com/talks/mike_matas.html. Totally awesome.

> ### TABLETS
>
> **YUP. WE'LL INSCRIBE** it in stone: Tablets are pretty damn cool. Hybrid computer, camera, TV, (soon-to-be phone?), GPS thingies. They're readers, writers, arithmetic keepers. Easier to schlep around than a laptop—you can even get work done on them. We love 'em. While the new Kindle Fire can light up your life for under $260, the iPad, with all its nifty apps and features, remains the most lust-worthy tablet on the market. But if it's an "add-on" to your basic electronic wardrobe, think about buying one used.

DISCONNECT TOGETHER

Gather the troops and get your entertainment the old-fashioned way. We're talking DVDs. School vacations, rainy weekends, and Saturday night at-home snuggle-fests are made better by family movie marathons. Pop some popcorn, stir up fruit-flavored spritzers and smoothies, spread pillows and blankets on the floor, press "play." Mix up movies and television. Do a sci-fi marathon: *Lost in Space, Star Trek, Star Wars, The Day the Earth Stood Still, The Matrix, Close Encounters of the Third Kind*. Watch the "big" pictures, the ones that go on forever that everyone will always remember: *Gone with the Wind, Gandhi, Chariots of Fire*. Teen flick classics by decade: *West Side Story, The Breakfast Club, Ferris Bueller's Day Off*.

Looking for more ideas? Our go-to source for all things movie: Rotten Tomatoes.

First stop: the public library for some free DVDs. Or find a Redbox in your neighborhood—for a little as a buck you can rent a top release for a night. Our favorite and most reliable video supplier is Netflix. Subscribing is a snap. For $7.99 a month you get unlimited instant video on demand. Hard-core DVD-watching family? Avoid being penny wise and pound foolish—while one disk a month will cost you $7.99, shell out the bucks for their next-tier pricing plan so you can rent more than one DVD at a time. If you're dying to see the next *Dexter* and it's not ready and waiting, you may become dangerous.

This is all a lot cheaper than buying four tickets to the movies, popcorn, and drinks, right?

MAKE A LITTLE MUSIC

Scour the family music libraries and make music playlists together. While your kids won't always appreciate your music and you may not always appreciate theirs (how did you get to be your mother?), model cross-generational music-appreciation respect.

Make it applicable to whatever you've got going on. Getting ready for a road trip to the Big Apple? Spend time gathering "New York, New York" covers across the decades: Frank Sinatra, Lou Reed, Rufus Wainwright, Jay-Z, U2, LCD Soundsystem. Watching *The Wizard of Oz*? Listen to renditions of "Somewhere over the Rainbow" by Judy Garland, Eva Cassidy, Israel "IZ" Ka'ano'i Kamakawiwo'ole, and Chet Baker.

Create a marching-band list or your favorite holiday songs list or a beat-the-blues list (for those days when nothing goes right). Curate a collection of the best music videos of all time. Start with your contributions: "Thriller" by Michael Jackson; "Take on Me" by A-Ha; "November Rain" by Guns N' Roses; "Weapon of Choice" by Fatboy Slim (classic Christopher Walken). Then have your kids add theirs. (Remember, no judging.)

Best idea of all? Make your own music.

Okay, we know most of you aren't down in the basement, mom on tambourines, dad on electric guitar, Junior on bass, Minnie on drums—but play around with Auto-Tune. There are scores (well, not really scores, but we liked the way it sounded) of great music-making programs for kids and adults, like GarageBand or MAGIX Music Maker 11 Deluxe.

Use the music to orchestrate family traditions. You don't have to be named Partridge to get your groove on. (Uh! Did we just write that?)

AN EXPLICIT PARENTAL WARNING

MUSIC AND VIDEO downloads are insidious little budget busters. A ring tone here, a new song or television episode there, and before you know it you (or they) have added to your monthly credit card bill *big*-time.

SPITTING IMAGES

When was the last time you updated the family camera? The photo program on your computer? Organized the pictures? (We know you have both boxes of old photos and one *huge* file on your computer.) Find footage of your kids as babies, toddlers, at their first dance recital, pitching the first ball game. Have you sat down with your kids and created slide shows? Videos? Web sites? Put music to pictures? Added text?

We just invested in the next generation of idiot cameras. This one is small enough to fit into our back pocket (barely) and it takes nearly professional-grade pictures. We've spent hours creating videos and slide shows on the computer: editing the frames, matching music, creating narratives. The possibilities are hilarious, dramatic, poignant, entertaining—and endless.

Have fun together.

The cost? After the camera—free.

TURN SOCIAL MEDIA INTO MULTIMEDIA

WE'VE BEEN USING a great tool called Storify to create what we think of as cross-media social-media collages. Mix and match original content (writing, photographs, video, music) with content you find across the Web—YouTube, news stories, music, *National Geographic*, *Car and Driver*, *Vogue* photos—whatever. Anything in the world is fair game. Make your own stories.

Creativity unleashed. It's simple. It's fun: http://storify.com.

YOU CAN'T BEAT THEM; JOIN THEM: OLD GAMES, NEW MEDIA

It's 2012. The ice guy is no longer hauling up big blocks to cool victuals, the horse isn't stabled in the barn, the mailperson is no longer delivering letters from faraway friends. Nothing stays the same and it's time to get into the game. We mean this literally: Play video games with your kids. No lecturing now on the evils of media distractions (you've heard plenty already). It's a part of life.

All three major systems (Wii from Nintendo, PlayStation 3 from Sony, Xbox Kinect from Microsoft) offer great features and opportunities for your family to play together. They also offer an interface to stream Web content or Netflix, and to connect with other online gamers (ah, you need to supervise the kiddies on this one). Embrace what you can do with it *together*.

Remember, there's a robust aftermarket for both the system and the games. If you're not yet a player, start by pricing out the real cost of getting a system. As with all electronic purchases, add-ons and doodads increase in price what at first glance seems a reasonable buy. As of this writing we like the Wii for entry-level gamers. It is the least expensive, plus Nintendo is the creator of Super Mario—and don't you have a bit of a weak spot in your heart for him? We've even come down off our high horse (see *Bitches on a Budget*) over the Wii Fit exercise games. Yes, we'll take real over artificial any day, but it's worth a try.

Sony's PlayStation 3 comes with a brand-new Blu-ray DVD player included in the cost of the system, has great graphics, and stores media.

The Xbox has the coolest technology; it's completely motion-sensitive, so you can play a game without using any controller at all. In this case, the base price is not the true price, making this the most expensive system when you finish adding in the cost of all the goodies you need.

Be smart. Always honor the rating systems. Always do your homework. Some games are hideously and disturbingly violent, misogynistic, and overly sexualized. Plus, if your kids are playing with strangers online you *must* monitor this. New boundaries mean new fun and new risks.

LET'S MAKE A DEAL

THIS IS A little like making a pact with the devil, but Microsoft developed this family guideline so you can make a contract with your child about your family's rules of play. It's not half-bad: http://www.getgamesmart.com.

A POSITIVE SPIN ON GAMES

"Everything in moderation" is a motto parents must hold near and dear as kids cycle through stages on their way to becoming who they are. We know it's tough to find balance. . . . Some activities are so absorbing, so fun, and so rewarding they border on being addictive (not just for the kids). Monitor the video game time but don't dis it. Because you know what? It's not all bad. There. We said it.

Think about this: We're not using carbon paper or Wite-Out anymore to reverse errors when we write. This allows for more risk, more creativity, more complex work (and more junk blogs blown into the ether). Everyone is a photographer or videographer, able to take hundreds of photos and manipulate them over and over again. The ability to try and try again is enabled by modern technology. (BTW, a random thought: While we're on the subject of risk, put this on the list of things to teach your kids—never fill out the address portion of an e-mail until the entire note is crafted.)

Look, there's a hell of a lot going on when your kids (or you) are playing the Sims, Portal, or Tactical Iraqi. Remember Freud? You know, the old Viennese guy with the cigar? He talked about repetition compulsion—about the drive to repeat activities until we master them and understand them. Well, he never played Grand Theft Auto, but we can apply his idea to video games. When you play these games, you get to try again and again to solve a problem. When you persevere, "game" the game, come at the same problem from different angles, you gain mastery. Unlike school, where risk and error can lead to long-term trouble, this universe is reversible. Games create narratives, tell stories. They put the players in experiences they may not be comfortable with. They invite players to assume fantasy personas. . . . Okay.

We'll stop now. But you get the point. In moderation, video games aren't all bad!

TED TALKS

TED IS A nonprofit dedicated to "ideas worth spreading." Check this out when you pay TED a visit: Jane McGonigal chatting up the benefits of video games (http://blog.ted.com/2010/03/17/gaming_can_make/).

BOUNDARIES BLOWN

We'll close with this thought from Google's online publication Think Quarterly: http://www.thinkwithgoogle.co.uk/quarterly/data/hal-varian-treating-data-obesity.html.

> "In 2010, the human race created 800 exabytes of information, from tweets and Facebook updates to PowerPoint presentations and photographs. That's 800 billion gigabytes, or the amount of data you can fit on 75 billion 16-gig iPads. To put that into context, between the dawn of civilization and 2003, we only created five exabytes; now we're creating that amount every two days. By 2020, that figure is predicted to sit at 53 zettabytes (53 trillion gigabytes)—an increase of 50 times."

That's some big data plan.

PART 6

THE WHOLE CHILD:
Run, Jump, Act, Sing, Dance, Camp—and Quit

INTRODUCTION

What if someone told you—before you had kids—about how your life would change? What if someone sat you down and patiently explained the overwhelming sense of responsibility, exhaustion, agitation? Surely it'd be the end of our species.

But no one tells you, or they try but can't get the point across, and you have kids anyway. You're here. They're here. You love them. You wouldn't do anything differently. Still, it's exhausting. From not touching a hot stove to not touching their privates in public to not touching car keys if they've had a drink: It's on you to instill the important messages so that later, *they* can make important decisions.

All along the way you want a teeny-tiny break from the responsibility, from all this parental power, but you can't get a break. And then suddenly they're old enough to make their own decisions, and you'd give anything to have a little power again. It's a no-win situation.

But it's not all exhaustion and responsibility, right? It's also fun and games and learning, right? Right. Except here, too, pressure rears its head. From ballet class to community service to camp, you feel pressure to pick the right program, the right sport, the right math supplement class, the right volunteer opportunity, or you're not a "perfect" mommy. They won't have the skills, tools, life experiences they need to successfully navigate in the world. The neighborhood kids will have a leg up: Noah will get the football scholarship, Juan the chemistry prize; Cerene will be first violin; Chrissy will win the World Championship of Public Speaking. And your little mini-me will be living at home and working at the corner fast-food joint salting fries. You'll do anything, pay any amount of money, sign them up for any enrichment, spend all your free time in the car to save him . . . right?

Hold on a sec.

TIME FOR THE ULTRASOUND—AND HAVE YOU THOUGHT ABOUT COLLEGE?

You know it starts young. Really young. The drive to enroll them in extracurricular lessons and programs is huge. Gymboree, Baby & Me, Tiny Tumblers. Then ballet class, judo, piano lessons. Volunteering at the shelter. Enrichment programs like early math circle, early foreign language immersion, creative kids' writing class, physics for fun . . .

Summer camp and specialty camps follow. Everyone you know has a child who's doing something interesting, and you're afraid your kid is going to be a lumpy schlemiel if you don't sign her up. *Now*.

Wait. Relax. Breathe. Before you head off to sign your kids up for music, math, and mambo boot camp, bear in mind that the best mom *balances* unstructured play and organized activities. The best mom does not outsource all the responsibility for enriching their lives. Just like charity begins at home, so do running and jumping and playing and singing and . . . you get the point.

Trust us on this: It's good for you, good for them, and *good for your budget*.

When you *do* sign them up for lessons and programs, you need a clear head and open eyes. You need to understand what is driving you to drive them across the county for fencing lessons; you need to listen to what they want; and you need to see them for who they are. Think of extracurricular games, lessons, programs, and camps as ways to broaden their interests, deepen skill sets, engage in different ways of learning, stay in shape, and (this is key) have fun. Help your kids grow into rich, whole, happy people!

30

A RADICAL IDEA:
Free Play

"Play is so important to optimal
child development that it has been recognized
by the United Nations High Commission
for Human Rights as a right of every child."

(http://www.aap.org/pressroom/playfinal.pdf)

Music to your ears? The "free" part or the "play" part? Both, we hope.

Busy parents, well-intentioned parents, worried parents, often fall into the habit of overstructuring their kids' lives under the misguided notion that more activities mean more enrichment. *After all,* they think, *isn't it better for James to be in drama class, soccer practice, and violin lessons than home watching TV and texting?* Or they believe that the more extracurriculars (i.e., the longer the résumé), the greater the chance to win the college sweepstakes.

The facts are that too much is just too much. A generation of hurried, car seat–strapped prisoners of overprogrammed parenting has come of age and is exhibiting the most depression, anxiety, and unhappiness of any recorded college class in the nation. Yeah. It's not going to be your kid, right? Trust us, it's a slippery slope: From overburdened parents passing kids from one activity

251

to another, to insecure parents caught in the keeping-up-with-the-Joneses parent trap, no one is immune. So remember:

- Kids need to be bored; they need to make their own fun; they need to call on their inner resources and explore.
- Free play builds the circuits in their brains to make connections across all disciplines.
- It teaches them to be original thinkers, to create, and to generate their own critical reasoning skills.
- To make this happen, you'll need to set rules and stick to them: for some set amount of time, no television, no computer, no plugging in or turning on. The cost? Consistency, patience, and mess.

HARDWIRED FOR PLAY

Playing and being playful begin at home. The hardwiring for *enjoying* living starts young. Have you ever wondered when the switch from play to exercise gets turned? What happens to the great storytellers, the uninhibited dancers, the joyful artists? How is it that kids naturally run around, play tag, bike, swing, jump off the couch, have fun, and stay in shape one day, and are heading for the dreaded treadmill chore the next? How is it that the little performer ends up zoned out watching reruns of *Gossip Girl* and *Law and Order: SVU*? (Oh, wait, that's you.)

Turn watching into acting. Disney costumes into creative dress-up. Boring computer games into interactive (live and in person) board games. It's their job to play and it's your job to help them.

DO IT TOGETHER

When they're young, get down and play with them. Build tower. Crash. Build tower. Crash. Build tower. Lobotomy. Yes, you'll enter Duplo hell after a while, but your tyke will love you for it forever. As kids get older, build Transformers, complex LEGO cities, model airplanes.

We're here to remind you that the old standbys are alive and well. Ramp up the card games, from go fish and crazy eights and gin to hearts and whist and bridge. Cut their teeth on Candy Land and Chutes and Ladders; move on to epic games of Monopoly and Risk. Do a monster jigsaw puzzle over time (in our family that would be years), or a crossword puzzle. Chess. Dominoes. Backgammon. Sudoku. Scrabble. Does it get any better? Any simpler? Any cheaper?

Set the stage by playing dress-up and charades with them; as they get older encourage them to act out tableaux with friends by carving out space for them to let their imaginations run wild. (Check your OCD at the door.) Go to the library and borrow plays, a history of theater, books on costumes. Organize the performances: Do it *with* your kids—get the cousins over, the neighbors, and their kids.

EDITH HEAD GAMES

KNOW WHO EDITH Head was? Only the most famous American costume designer of all time—beloved by Audrey Hepburn, Natalie Wood, Elizabeth Taylor. Teach your kids about her glamorous legacy and help them make their own costumes. Give them each a few bucks to scour Goodwill. Dig through the attic. Lend your own scarves, heels, costume gems. Dare them to make a splash onstage, and photograph them in dramatic poses. (At their wedding, you'll have a slide show guaranteed to bring the house down.)

GET MOVING

Channel your inner athletic goddess, and be their first fit role model. Shut down the computers, iPads, Kindles, and Nooks. Turn off the iPhones and BlackBerries (see Part V, "Technomoms"), leave the load of laundry, and slide that stack of bills into the drawer. Now go out. Swing on the playground, cycle around the neighborhood, dance together, play catch, hike, window-shop (briskly). Take advantage of your town recreation facilities and bat balls on the tennis court, swim in the pool, ice-skate on the rink.

Outside of the equipment—it's all free.

HOMEGROWN

THERE WAS A time kids went to school and came home and helped on the family farm, or in the family shop, or with the cooking and cleaning and child raising. When kids were seen and not heard. When there was no discussion about where they wanted to go on vacation or what they liked to eat. Yes, there was a time before the business of influencing kids to influence mom to buy stuff accounted for a billion dollars in food sales. A time long ago, before we became obsessed with pleasing them and keeping them happy all of the time.

Don't get us wrong! We're not advocating for the seen-and-not-heard, conscripted-child-labor days of yore. But just like the early days of the women's movement threw stay-at-home moms under the bus, programmed enrichments have wrongly delegitimized basic homely activities.

Mama, there is high value in low-cost, old-fashioned "extracurriculars." In the food chapter, we planted the seeds for a victory garden; we got the fire going for them to be cooking. In the shopping chapter: sewing, knitting, woodworking. Think about formally and informally instilling the pleasures of home arts and crafts into their lives.

Need more supervision, organization, skill sets? Outsourcing is allowed. Think about the Brownies. Cub Scouts. Girl Scouts. Boy Scouts. 4-H.

SWING LO-CAL

Playgrounds are free and fun, and a great place to meet other families with their kids. Duh. If you're a SAHM, make it your daily business to go to your local playground. (If you're a working mom, go on the weekends.) *You* do whatever Georgia does—

swing to the sky, swoop down slides, groan through chin-ups on the monkey bars. Chat it up with other moms and dads. Join with them and their kids in games. Find interesting playgrounds nearby; take day trips to check out dinosaur slides, pirate ships, and tree houses.

KEEP GROWING AND PLAYING

Find age-neutral sports to do together, like Rollerblading, swimming, bicycling. Teach your kids about being risk takers and lifelong learners; start a new sport along with them. Learn to sail. Learn to ice-skate. Take up skiing—water or snow. Show them how, with time, your initial clumsiness becomes competence becomes—maybe?—mastery. Fall, laugh, pick yourself up. They'll internalize the lesson.

Hike. Make it a family goal to climb all the local peaks. Look at the elevations on a map; begin by climbing small hills; as they (and you) become fitter, tackle higher mountains. Little kids are born scientists! Turn the hikes into discovery adventures. How about scat hunting? (Really, what eight-year-old is not delighted by poop?) Google Images provides more pictures of animal poop than you'll care to see. Or check in at the local bird sanctuary and learn to make real cuckoo sounds.

Not nature lovers? Do urban walks: river walks, historic walks, fund-raising walks. Take an architectural tour on foot through your own hometown.

What if you live in a cold-weather climate? Does the day seem to end when the sun sets, and playing outside is not an option? Or do you live in an area where it's not safe to shoo your kid out the door? Or you don't have a backyard? Stock up on jump ropes, stationary bikes (put theirs up on an indoor trainer), hula hoops.

Need more activity? No need to join a pricey club. Visit the local Y, community center, or Boys & Girls Club, and send them up the climbing wall, rolling down the bowling alley, spinning in the woods.

No money is no excuse.

A BACKYARD REVIVAL

TIME TO SLOW it all down. Save your sanity. Shut your purse. Have some fun. Organize backyard games for kids of all ages. Whip up some G&Ts for the parents (or grab some Pabst Blue Ribbon—you're on a budget, after all), and send the kiddos out to flex their muscles. Set up a couple of sprinklers, roll out a Slip 'N Slide. Hand them potato sacks and set them racing. Chalk a four-square box on your driveway. Hang a tetherball on a sturdy tree branch. A little imagination and easy labor can turn your backyard into a low-tech wonderland. Dodgeball, anyone? Tug-of-war? Jump-rope contest? Hula hoop spectacular?

Crank up some music and light some tiki torches as dusk descends. Old-school activities are the new Wii.

31

THE ROAD MAP:
A Balanced Approach
to Wholeness

Yes, free play is critical and budget-friendly, and kids need more of it than they're getting. But they *also* need structured activities. Participating in well-organized and well-run arts and sports programs enhances creative and cognitive skills. Kids need a place to take *un*graded risks, work at something over and over again to achieve mastery, succeed (and fail) outside the judgment of a classroom. Face it, not every eleven-year-old kid is a rocket scientist in school—but he may be a pinball wizard outside of it.

Great extracurricular programming:

- helps kids find their voice
- connects them to mentors outside of school
- leads to improved self-esteem and better academic performance
- teaches them to work collaboratively

• teaches them how to give and receive growth-enhancing critiques. (Trust us, knowing how to balance empty praise while offering self-esteem-building criticism is one of the challenges of modern parenting.)

SLASH! SLASH! SLASH!

Hear that? It's the sound of you screaming at a Guns N' Roses concert in 1990.

It's *also*—unfortunately—the sound of programs being cut.

In this day of muni budget cutting, lots of schools can no longer afford sports, music, theater, art. But these activities help broaden kids' thinking skills, bring texture and pleasure to living, instill healthy habits, and offer exposure to real-life career paths. As lovely, talented, and smart as you are, there are experts who bring professional skill and talent to teaching these subjects.

Plus, let's be real: Structured extracurriculars fill a void. You're at work, no one else is home to play with them, and they're safer in a supervised setting than running around your neighborhood.

Your job? To find worthwhile programs for your kids to participate in, and to do this in a way that doesn't break the bank, burden your psyche, or burn them out.

YOU'RE DRIVING THEM. WHAT'S DRIVING YOU?

Before you spend the money to enroll them, before you buy expensive equipment, before you commit valuable time (your kids' and yours), evaluate *what is driving you*. Understand your hopes, anxieties, biases, and parenting style, so that you can meet your children's needs, not yours. Then listen carefully to what they want, see who they are, and think about what they need. Don't ignore their voices! For God's sake, you want to save Johnny the expense of therapy in later years (this is a money book, after all).

THE MOMMY DIAGNOSTIC: WHO ARE YOU?

THE INSECURE MOM: EVERYONE'S DOING IT. . . .

Little Max's friends are all signing up for a judo class for five-year-olds two towns over that meets at six thirty on Wednesday night. Never mind that Max has expressed no interest in judo; you're afraid he'll be the odd man out at recess if he doesn't share this bonding experience. So, quick—you need to pay for the class. You need to buy him a new white judo outfit. You need to organize a carpool. You need to interrupt dinner. You need to drag your other kids out and entertain them while he takes his lessons. Uh, you need to say no.

THE FRUSTRATED MOM: YOU COULD HAVE BEEN A CONTENDER. . . .

You spent your childhood in dance classes. It was your favorite part of your day, week, year, life. You had Sugar Plum Fairy dreams every night. Once you even got to dance with the nearby professional ballet company in their cast of *Nutcracker* thousands. Then puberty set in. You grew and grew some more, taller and taller, wider and wider, and so ended your prima ballerina dreams. Slight and slender Sam loves soccer. Kicking the ball. Yelling and screaming. Being part of the team. You argue that Sam will bring a more graceful and athletic nimbleness to the soccer game if she takes ballet class. Sam says no. You say yes. We say no. (If you need a stronger argument, rent *Black Swan*.)

THE LET-IT-BE MOM: WAKE UP AND
HEAR THE MUSIC. . . .

Jeremy listens to music all day long. He never stops humming, bobbing his head to rhythms you can't hear. In his spare time he uses computer programs to create original compositions. Teachers comment on his natural gifts. You're tone-deaf, overscheduled, and can barely get dinner on the table—let alone add in another driving commitment. Yet you are nagged by the feeling that his needs aren't being met. It's time to find a local music school that teaches music theory.

THE COMPETITIVE MOM: JUST THIS
ONE LITTLE EXTRA . . .

Corrie and her friends do gymnastics four days a week. On Saturdays they all go to creative movement to enhance their dance moves. On Sunday they go to strength-training class. Now a number of her tumbling pals have hired private coaches to work on individual routines. You already send her to specialty gym camp in the summer; now your stomach is in knots trying to figure out how to afford one more activity before Megan or Sophie get a leg up on your budding Olympian. We say imagine what these poor *kids'* stomachs are like! Stand down, mama. It's time to subtract—not add—activities from her crazy, overprogrammed life.

THE DELUDED MOM: HUH?

Have you signed your daughter up for harpsichord lessons at the age of seven because someone told you the most selective colleges recruit to fill slots? You figure that every big school orchestra needs a harpsichordist and, since you haven't seen any other kids schlepping a harpsichord around the neighborhood, it's your opportunity to get her onto the bandwagon early. Never mind that she's a tiny tomboy with no musical interest *whatsoever*. And you're thinking this is clever strategic thinking? Ah. More like scrambled thinking.

BE A CLEAR-EYED YO-YO-MAMA

Every mama should be looking at her little one through rose-colored glasses. That's what mamas are for! Yet you also need a set of cool blue lenses to see whom they're performing for, what they're really learning, and how much you're investing in time, money, and expectations. Trust us, it's easy to get carried away when little Patience stands up at her recital, the first in the class to master the cello piece, and the instructor, with eyes closed, smiles and nods as he sways to her music. We know you'll be first in line signing her up for the early string quartet.

What mom wouldn't burst with pride when Paul dunks the ball to win the town tourney and the coach grabs her to say that in all his years of coaching he's never seen a kid play like him?

We know you're thrilled. You should be. What we *also* know is that a parent's overenthusiastic response can smother a child's pleasure in playing. And we know a teacher's praise can overinflate a parent's expectations and underinflate her bank account. So whether it's the cello or basketball, balance is the game. Yes, there are prodigies. You may have the next Jacqueline du Pré or Kevin Garnett in your midst. But chances are, if you invest too much too soon, they will not play for themselves, but to please you. This is costly in several ways.

The point here? *Know who you are* so you can see them for who they are. Balance your kids' needs with your own needs—and learn to tell the difference.

EYEWITNESS

ONCE YOU THINK hard about who they are (as opposed to who *you* would like them to be), on a rare occasion you might even have an epiphany about what they should be doing.

We did. Once.

We call it our only moment of parental clarity. We had an I-don't-want-to-take-a-risk-and-do-anything-new kind of girl when she was small. She hated any kind of sport, but had great fine-motor skills. She also had the most annoying habit of banging, tapping, clapping, slamming her feet and hands on everything she could—all in syncopated rhythm. We encouraged her to try the drums. Her response was no. Did we listen? No. We found a program nearby and the teacher agreed to meet with her once.

We pushed her. Really bad mama. Truth be told, we kind of dragged her from the house kicking and screaming to the lesson. We waited outside as she and the teacher met. She walked out with a set of drumsticks and the biggest smile on her face ever. She played drums all the way through high school, eventually forming an all-girl band.

She rocked.

THE MYTH OF THE RENAISSANCE CHILD

You want your kid to become dynamic, active, happy: whole. You know a convergence of many experiences helps makes this happen. Every child has an individual arc of social and physical development, and your job is to expose him or her to a broad range of activities to meet his or her needs at any given stage. First ask her what she would like to do—but recognize that kids don't always know what they don't know. (Remember the drummer.) Then seek advice: Consult with your pediatrician about age-appropriate choices, solicit ideas from teachers, ask friends with older children. Learn from others' successes and mistakes.

DO SOME HONEST ACCOUNTING

Remember, many overprogrammed kids lose their joy in playing (or lose sleep at night) from packing too much into busy lives. Consider: How long is their school day? What commitments are nonnegotiable in your family? Religious school? Language classes? Volunteering/community service?

Sit down with them at the beginning of each season and make a plan. The guiding principle should be "sound mind, sound body." Balance the desire to give them broad exposure to different activities with the budget you have allocated. Do not let them do too much at one time: one major commitment a season. Keep it simple.

As they grow, encourage them to try different arts and sports. Mix individual and group activities. Say Selena's signed up for a play that promises to be all-consuming; make sure she gets out on her Rollerblades or takes a run once in a while. Since the play has a cast of thousands, maybe this is the time to sample an individual sport on the weekend, like an introductory yoga or golf class. Golf? Some kids actually like it—although we can't get the point of chasing a little ball around the field with a club. (But see? We're willing to leave our prejudices at the door. You can, too.). Or keep the weekends blessedly free until the play ends. When she's taken her last curtain call, encourage her to try an individual activity.

WAKE UP AND LISTEN TO THIS ONE

ACCORDING TO DR. Avi Sadeh of Tel Aviv University, for every hour of lost sleep, a child loses two years of cognitive maturation. So a sleep-deprived fifth grader could be working at the third-grade level.

SIT DOWN AND LISTEN TO THIS ONE

THE EDINA, MINNESOTA, high school shifted its morning start time from seven twenty-five to eight thirty a.m. The impact was immediate and measurable. The top 10 percent of the class SAT scores had been averaging 1288. The year of the shift, the average SAT score for the top 10 percent of the class was 1500. This stunning increase the educators attribute to more sleep.

PLANNING THE ROUTE

How do you go about finding the right violin teacher, ballet class, sports team and league?

BE NOSY

Get referrals. Start at school by tapping the music, gym, or art teacher. Ask friends in the neighborhood or at church or synagogue. Get the good, the bad, and the ugly. Ask what they like about the teacher or the program. Ask what they would like them to be better at. Ask what programs or instructors they've had bad experiences with and why (and avoid them).

THE TORTOISE OR THE HARE

THE EXTRACURRICULAR PRIZE often goes to the tortoise: the child who finds something he loves doing and continues at it year after year, for his own pleasure—not to win the race, but because he loves doing it.

STRAIGHT FROM THE HORSE'S MOUTH

Talk to the leader, in person or on the phone. Ask about her philosophy of teaching or coaching. What's required of her students? How much practice time? Are there costly music books or art materials in your future? Can you have a trial period? If it's a bad match, what is her refund policy? Ask how many students she has and how long on average they have been with her. Ask for referrals. It's easy to get carried away by an instructor's credentials, but just because they played saxophone in the Chicago Symphony Orchestra, it doesn't mean that they will be good at teaching ten-year-olds.

EYE SPY

Schedule a time to watch the ice hockey practice, the skating lessons, the music school's recital, the acting class. Are the kids engaged? Active participants? Happy? Are the teachers or coaches respectful, engaged, enjoying their job? Remember, when your kid is starting out in a new activity at the beginner level, this should be fun. It should be instructional. Everyone should be playing.

LIGHTEN THE LOAD

Ask about pricing. Don't be shy. Everyone's doing it. Ask whether there's a discount for multiple lessons or multiple kids. Ask about withdrawal policies, illness, and makeup classes. Ask about semi-private rather than private lessons as a way to save money.

MONEY MATTERS

GET CREATIVE WHEN it comes to paying for programming!

First, there is no shame in asking for help. Youth leagues often have scholarships or discounted rates for families with need. Organizations like the Police Athletic League, youth orchestras, theaters, Rotary and civic clubs may offer scholarships. Professional sports teams often underwrite programs for kiddos in their towns.

Then ask yourself, what do *you* have to give? Consider trading time with the local ice rink, art school, karate club: answer phones, send out mailings, or update Web sites in exchange for discounted or free lessons.

THE EXTRACURRICULAR CURRICULUM

Academically oriented after-school programs come in all shapes and sizes: remedial programs, enrichment programs, exploration programs, crafting-little-genius programs. Some kids need a boost in a subject, some families want their child to learn a language that is meaningful for the family, some kids have a wild passion for a subject, and some moms believe it's their duty to nurture a budding interest right away or they're not being "good" moms.

Clearly, a child struggling in a subject needs help. Don't

ignore this. Work with the school. Is there help available during school time or in an after-school program? Are there exercises and assignments you can do with them? (Although, math after fifth grade was all Greek to us.) If that's not enough, you might have to spring for an outside tutor (see Khan Academy below). Ask around at school. Often teachers, already familiar with the curriculum, tutor in the neighborhood. Before you sign up, talk to a family the teacher has worked with and make sure he was helpful. Finally, make sure you're putting your money into a winning proposition. Sometimes it's a bad match. Listen to your child. If your kiddo complains or seems bored or doesn't show improvement, trust him. No passivity allowed. Find someone else.

Thinking of adding an extra academic activity for a child who's already thriving? Okay, as long as it's something *she* really wants to do. Aspiring writers and poets may want to try a mini writing group. Debaters might want to join the forensic team (wear them out before they get home). Others might be interested in mixing materials in the chemistry lab. All good. The caution: Keep it simple. Save your energy. Don't extinguish a kid's interest by blowing up a passing fancy into an after-school chore.

THE FUN FACTOR?

We had friends who had mathematical whiz kids. They signed them up for after-school math circle (sounds like one of the circles of hell to us, but, hey, we write). At the end of a long day of grade school, they'd pick them up and schlep them over to the world's greatest university to meet with a math professor to do number gymnastics. Yes, their minds were stretched, but when did these little ones get to stretch their limbs?

Keep it age-appropriate—there's a big difference between a high school kid enthusiastically competing in the academic College Bowl and a second grader doing algorithms when he still could be kicking the ball or throwing clay.

KHAN ACADEMY: Free Learning

SALLY STRUGGLING IN Algebra II? Jimmy getting ready for the SAT exam? Manny hungering to move ahead in physics?

Before you spend a penny on a pricey tutor or special enrichment, check out www.khanacademy.org. This is the most awesome site on the Internet. Find thousands of videos and scores of self-paced exercises—from simple arithmetic to complex math to physics to history to finance. (More subjects and tutorials are being added all the time.)

Started by Sal Khan to help his cousins with algebra, this incredible site has grown exponentially. The organizers describe the site as "a not-for-profit with the goal of changing education for the better by providing a free world-class education to anyone anywhere."

Be smart. Save money. Take a course yourself.

GET INTO THE GAME: SPORT AND FITNESS

WORK OUT A FRAMEWORK FOR LIFELONG MOVEMENT: PLAY BEFORE PAY

It's not news that the entire kiddie-perfecting complex is enrichment obsessed and program driven. You're sure to be a no-good, terrible, very bad mom if Alexander isn't signed up for a town sport team each and every season, or Kelsey doesn't begin gymnastics in kindergarten, or Lindsay doesn't play town *and* travel soccer *and* attend summer soccer camp *and* all the regional specialty soccer clinics.

Relax. This is not the only way for kids to stay in shape.

According to the Centers for Disease Control and Prevention, children and adolescents should be *physically active for at least one hour each day*. This activity should cover aerobics, muscle-strengthening, and bone-strengthening exercise. Moderate and vigorous aerobic activity should account for most of the daily sixty minutes, while at least three times a week attention should be focused on muscle- and bone-strengthening activities.

The good news for a busy, wallet-sensitive mom? Most of the activities the CDC recommends are easily accomplished. Hiking, biking, hopping, skipping, jumping rope—all are good. As are bicycling, running, tennis, swinging. Even house- and yard work will keep kids fit.

If you live in an area where it's safe to walk or ride their bikes to school, get them out the door on time. No whining that they're tired. No excuses that it's raining (buy an umbrella).

Keep them moving.

GET DRAFTED OR SIGN UP AND JOIN THE TEAM

Don't misunderstand. We're not saying organized sports are bad; we're just saying that there are loads of ways for kids to stay in shape. They don't need to be part of a pay-for-play effort to stay fit. Nor do they need to be athletic perfectionists and best in class to enjoy playing the game.

Organized kids' sports offer meaningful benefits beyond the obvious athletic ones—life lessons like resiliency, cooperation, strategy, endurance. They learn about winning and losing and trying again. Kids who successfully manage sports and academics develop great organizational and time-management strategies that serve them well in later life. Plus, with so many kids participating in organized after-school activities, a sports program may be the only place a kid gets to socialize.

USE IT AGAIN

WHAT DO YOU think happens to all those outgrown hockey skates, skis, lacrosse sticks?

Buy hand-me-down and used. Organize an activities swap day in your community. Go to PlayItAgainSports.com. Use craigslist. Look into the Freecycle Network. Post signs at the local library.

Beg, borrow, and steal, and you won't go bankrupt on uniforms and equipment. No snobbery, no I-need-it-all-new-and-shiny bull**** allowed.

Don't forget to ask your child to help you brainstorm and to contribute to the search. Doing this as a family helps you save money, teaches creative thinking and environmental awareness, and helps your child to take ownership of the activity.

BEFORE HORMONES RAGE

BEAR IN MIND that preadolescent children are physically and developmentally different from teens. The American Academy of Pediatrics says, "Organized sports programs for preadolescents should complement, not replace, the regular physical activity that is a part of free play, child-organized games, recreational sports, and physical education programs in the schools." We believe that little kids' sports teams should not be awarding trophies and holding banquets that put undue emphasis on winning. These are adult values, and are not appropriate for teaching kids to take joy in the process of playing. Run, don't walk, away.

A SMORGASBORD OF OPTIONS

When your child is ready, give him or her a broad taste of activities to find what resonates. Don't force a kid who doesn't love soccer to keep at it. Maybe he hates running up and down the field, fears getting his shin kicked—*honor this!* Give another sport a try. You don't have a David Beckham on your hands, but who's to say he's not the next Babe Ruth?

Or you may have a kid who just doesn't like team sports. So what? We're not really team players either. It doesn't mean she's a misanthrope. She can stay healthy and exercise lots of ways: skateboarding, running, bowling, swimming, martial arts.

No gender assumptions allowed (meaning you should reread the above paragraphs and switch pronouns, okay?). Just because you have a girl doesn't mean she might not like to give rugby or football a go. Your son might want to try his toes at ballet—hey, Rahm Emanuel won a scholarship to the Joffrey Ballet but turned it down to attend Sarah Lawrence (a school with an outstanding dance program). Now he's the mayor of a sweet, easygoing city called . . . Chicago.

WHO'S THE COACH?

Youth teams depend on volunteers. Need we say more? The operative word here is *volunteer*. You get what you pay for. Some are bad; some are great. No national accrediting program oversees your local town's volunteer sports coaches. While you'll find some national standards like the National Alliance for Youth Sports (http://nays.intrafusiontech.com/CMSContent/File/National_Standards08FINAL(2).pdf), there's no single formal training or guideline checklist for youth coaches. So be nosy and check around town before you send your kid off to play.

Or, better yet, volunteer and do it right (we know you can).

BE HEADSTRONG—IT'S NOT A SPLURGE IF IT KEEPS THEM SAFE

NO SHORTCUTS WHEN it comes to safety gear. Buy the best you can afford.

Don't send kids out with equipment that's not in good condition.

If you have a child playing football, for example, look into the latest in technology from Xenith helmets.

WE'VE SCREWED UP (SO YOU DON'T HAVE TO)

We're not athletic, so we wanted our kids to have skills we didn't have. Our goal was to expose them to many different kinds of sports.

Swimming was number one on the list. We took our oldest as a toddler to a program that had us throw her in the water to sink or swim. Guess what happened? We took her twice but the hysteria wasn't worth it—for either of us. We quit. We tried again when she was older. The local high school pool offered lessons. She had a series of terrific instructors, and loved it, and even ended up on their swim team.

We also signed our kids up for local youth league teams. We had good and bad experiences—including the frightening coach with the faux-English accent who wore an ascot under his polo jersey and ran around in short shorts, whistle plugged into his mouth, and who refused to let any child on the field who didn't already know how to play soccer. Yes, these were eight-year-olds. We were certain that the *Candid Camera* team was filming.

What we found on the town teams was a lot of politics. Good and bad coaching. Rabid parents. Absent parents. Normal

parents. Insane parents who yelled at their kids for making errors, yelled at other kids for making errors, yelled at the umps
for making errors. We learned to trust our instincts and also to
trust our kids. If they swore they were having fun (even though
we couldn't bear the ascot, short shorts, and attitude), we didn't
stop them.

SPORTS AND THE EXTRACURRICULAR
COLLEGE SWEEPSTAKES

Urban legends abound about how to get your children into the
college of *your* dreams. Kids need to get straight As, play multiple sports, speak multiple languages, star in the school play,
start their own social networking site, volunteer at a homeless
shelter—no, *solve* the problem of homelessness in their town.

We won't lie: The formula for entry to the fifteen to twenty-
five top competitive schools is secret and shifting. One year they
need scientists; the next the focus is on computer science majors,
the following year Arabic majors.

We do know this: The sports recruiting card is a tricky
gambit. Who's to say the dream college's hockey team needs a
forward the year of your Wayne Gretzky's application?

There are no guarantees. We know a young man who was
well on his way in hockey, recruited by every powerhouse team
and prestigious academic institution. He and his parents spent
his entire childhood on the ice, shuttling between four a.m. practices and weekend games and special summer camps. December
of his senior year, he broke his leg in three places. Every college
that had wooed him withdrew its support.

Your kid should play a sport for the love of the sport, stay
focused in school and get good grades, stay well-rounded. Don't
let her miss her childhood. It happens only once.

LOOK CLOSER

CONTACT THE *BIG* guys nearby. Whether it's an NFL team or minor-league baseball franchise, they'll often partner with local communities to offer clinics and instruction.

Contact the association for the sport. For example, the United States Tennis Association has a robust Web site that offers everything from up-to-date rules to the best equipment to a "finder" for a program near you.

Contact local civic organizations and private clubs to see whether they offer scholarships for kids in their communities.

More resources to find programs near you:

- American Youth Football
- BlazeSports
- Boys & Girls Clubs of America
- Dixie Baseball
- National Recreation and Park Association
- National PTA
- National Sports Center for the Disabled
- Police Athletic League
- United States Golf Association
- United States Tennis Association
- Women's Sports Foundation

Okay, sweaty enough? Enough raw, pumping adrenaline for the moment? Great. Take a sip of Gatorade (no, actually, don't—that's a waste of $$) and a deep breath.

There are more aspects to building a whole child, like art and music and drama and . . .

32

THE ARTS ON YOUR WATCH:
Teaching Appreciation
(with Minimal Subcontracting)

It can be harder for kids to jump into the arts than into sports. Think about it: Does your town have a pottery league or painting team or flute ensemble that everyone in the neighborhood signs up for? Is there an arts equivalent to the Olympics that inspires kids to become great painters or writers or opera singers? Sports are easy to join. Sports are "cool." Everyone basically knows what's available.

It takes more work—for both you and your kids—to forge a real connection to the arts.

And it's just as important.

Our world is digital, wired, dynamic. Kids will need a range of flexible skills to succeed. The convergence of words, images, sound, and motion demands conceptual thinkers and problem solvers able to make connections across disciplines. In short, they'll need to think broadly.

Instilling a lifelong appreciation for the arts begins in your home court—and it doesn't cost a lot.

> ## THE COMMUNITY CENTER
>
> **MAKE IT YOUR** business to investigate what is going on inside the nearest community arts center. Bet you haven't done this yet. Most likely, they offer everything from theater and music to pottery and painting to dance and yoga. Make this your first stop in affordable local arts enrichment.

OPEN YOUR EARS

Is your musical repertoire limited? Mozart before your time? The Beatles quaint oldies? Puccini a fab pop-art designer? If Michael Jackson and Counting Crows are your musical touchstones, then listen up: Open your ears and start exposing yourself and the young'uns to the greats. Just like charity begins at home, so does music appreciation.

When you're in the car, buckle up, shut off the DVD, and start the music. *Do not* allow your car to become a rolling nursery or, later on, a sugar-pop machine. The car is your bully pulpit. Use all that driving time as an opportunity to indoctrinate your kid in the music you love (or want to learn about). And let her push back. Let a musical dialogue unfold.

Play those sound tracks you've created from all those overperformed musicals: *Grease, Les Mis, Rent, Sweeney Todd*. (The library should have a good stock.) Trust us: They'll be hooked, and before you know it, you'll have a regular *High School Musical* happening with each car ride.

Opera fan? No? Why not? Start with *La Bohème, Carmen, The Barber of Seville*. Grab CDs at the library. Later on you can bring them to the show.

Folk music? Every kid needs an angsty, socially righteous soul. Turn on Ani DiFranco, Joni Mitchell, Leonard Cohen, Dylan.

Get on the jazz train with Miles Davis, Billie Holiday, Stan Getz, Astrud Gilberto, Thelonious Monk.

Rap and R & B? Think Beyoncé. Kanye. De La Soul. Make sure lyrics are age-appropriate. Make it up yourselves. Raise poets. Play the Beatles' *White Album*, then Jay-Z's *Black Album*. Then expose them to the *Grey Album*, DJ Danger Mouse's classic mash-up of the two. (Preview first—some tracks contain rough language.) Your kids will be impressed.

Expose them to various instruments. Do a run on the best riffs on guitar: Chuck Berry's "Johnny B. Goode"; Jimi Hendrix's "Purple Haze"; Cream's "Crossroads." Then move on to keyboard, violin, etc.

Check out the library's world music collection (no one else is). Do South American one week, African the next, then Indian ragas.

Not sure where to start? There're cheaper alternatives than randomly downloading everything iTunes suggests onto your iPod. C'mon, have you forgotten about that excessively pierced know-it-all behind the counter of the music store? Trust us: He'll be more than happy to help.

STILL LOST LOOKING FOR LESSONS?

YOUR LOCAL COMMUNITY center comes up short in the kiln, paint, and viola departments. The kids' school isn't offering. The neighbors don't have a nice word to say about anyone who's taught their kid (okay, they're crabby and don't have a nice word to say about you, your kid, or your dog). No one you know ever needed a French horn teacher.

Call the big institutions in your area. Art institute. Philharmonic. Ballet. Is there a local college with a conservatory? Maybe its teachers are pricey, but the students aren't. Check in with the nearest art college. Maybe it offers youth classes, or there's a poor graduate student who can teach your kid manga.

WE HEART ART

Make going to the local museums part of your weekend routine—a particularly welcome relief when weather is extreme. Many museums offer special kids' classes and programs: scavenger hunts, family arts carts with puzzles and textile projects, drawing programs in the galleries, artists' demonstrations.

Make a game out of what you see. How many colors of blue are there in that Picasso painting? Can you find the head, arm, horse? Do you think the artist liked the man he painted? What do you think it would be like to be a kid in the nineteenth century? Could you imagine sitting on that sofa, bed, chair? Check out killer eighteenth-century boots in the costume galleries; find to-die-for gold necklaces in the Egyptian wing; decide who in the family the Maori masks resemble. Wow, look at the ornate filigree work in that sterling silver teapot. . . . Okay, that may be pushing it! But you can teach a lot more than just about the silver teapot. Think about it: Paul Revere was a master silversmith and one of the founding fathers. What a great Renaissance man role model in our age of superspecialization.

SPECTATE

GO TO PLAYS, concerts, and dance performances. Just like in sports, the amateurs are cheaper than the pros. Attend low-cost local high school and college performances. Watch your paper boy deliver a monologue. Younger kids always look up to older kids—their real hero's not LeBron James but James Spinnacker, the teenage saxophonist down the block. Support your neighbors' kids, your nieces and nephews, by heading to their modern dance recital, poetry reading, photography opening. Find kids' classics like *Peter and the Wolf* and *The Nutcracker*. Once they've become excited spectators, splurge on a Broadway show. Or go to a rock concert (while they'll still be seen with you).

DANCE, PLAY, SHOOT, SING ALONG

Don't forget about dance and theater. Go. Watch. Participate. You might be surprised by what's available in your area. For instance, the Family Y in Los Alamos offers belly dance, kathak, and Bharatanatyam dance classes (East Indian and South Indian classical dance) for all ages. The Madison Area YMCA in New Jersey offers swing, tap, Latin, and jazz classes you can take with your high school son or daughter.

Dance combines physical prowess with creative movement. Don't limit this powerful experience to girls. Make sure your boys get to try as well!

Work on an amateur production with your kids. Just think of the benefits: The kiddos get to see you in a whole different way (not yelling and screaming). It's yet another way to show (rather than tell) them that learning is a lifelong venture. Rather than just sitting and waiting for them in the car, you'll actually be in the action. Remember, moms deserve to have fun, too.

STOP TIME

Buy great cameras the whole family can use. While most of the time we're freaking out about the time we all spend plugged in and wired, the creative possibilities opened by digital cameras and photography are limitless. Take a class together. Get a project started. (See Part V, "Technomoms.")

33

VOLUNTEERING/COMMUNITY SERVICE:
Get the Good On

Who doesn't have a hot button? Something that just gets your goat. You know, the holier-than-thou Prius owner who's always on her high horse about the environment and waste? She also has a weekend ski house, a Range Rover, and never recycles her water bottles. There's something wrong with the picture.

Our hot button? The volunteer and service imperative that has become just another box that kids check off on their way . . . somewhere. The one imposed by school, church, mosque, or synagogue; the one that conventional wisdom says they must do to get into the college of their choice; the one that parents obey by outsourcing their kids to programs in order to teach empathy; the one clueless people (like the harpsichord mom) spend thousands of dollars on when they send kids to exotic places to help the "natives."

We believe in kindness, caring, and helping. Helping should come from the heart. (Okay. That's way sappier than our normal snarky selves, but this is our hot button.) Your job is both to be a role model and to give them opportunities to see the effect of their work in real ways that touch them. We don't think their savings should be tithed to charity (see page 176 in chapter 23: Teaching Money).

We also believe there's plenty of do-gooding to be done close to home, whether it's sitting with an aging grandparent or bringing groceries to a neighbor or restocking books at a library. Just like your kids don't need to go to NYC to take ballet classes, they don't need to go to Johannesburg to be helpful to someone else. There are hundreds of opportunities to help nearby.

We wrote in *Bitches on a Budget* about volunteering: "Make it fun. Nothing should feel all serious and penance-like." Start by bringing the kids with you. Some kids will love the stacking of food in a pantry. Others will love serving in a soup kitchen. Still others might like planning a garden or volunteering on a political campaign (yes, a kind of important service, being engaged in the political process), or dishing kibble at the animal shelter. Encourage kids to find their own passion, and share it in whatever way feels right.

Teach them there are people in need in our communities. To borrow a faded bumper sticker: Think globally; act locally.

YOU MAY NOT PAY TO GIVE

DO NOT PAY to send your child away to a camp to do community service. Period.

Kids can volunteer at the animal shelter, an assisted-living facility, the church, the temple, a soup kitchen. The opportunities are endless in your own backyard.

More on volunteering:

Volunteer Match: www.volunteermatch.org

Charity Navigator (to learn more about an organization before you sign up or give): www.charitynavigator.org

34

HELLO, MOTHER. HELLO, FATHER:
Camp on a Budget

While the kids can hardly wait for the last day of school, often parents go into freakout mode wondering what they're going to do come summer. Whether you're a working mom worrying about supervision or an at-home mom cringing at the thought of scuffling siblings and endless exclamations of, "I'm bored"—pay attention. We've got a few ideas.

Camps, sleepaway and otherwise, come in all shapes and sizes. Day camp, overnight camp, morning sessions, eight-week sessions, music, baseball, gymnastics, space, business, soccer, math—the list goes on. Think beyond bug juice and gimp. These days, camps are big business.

THE LONG AND SHORT OF IT

Lots of adults say camp was their happiest childhood experience: color wars, panty raids, necking behind the mess hall. For these parents, sending kids to overnight camp feels like a rite of

284

passage. Of course, kids' attitudes vary widely: For some going away to camp is a dream; for others it's a nightmare.

Start with what your child likes to do, then figure out the right formula for your family. Despite your hatred of all things color war, a traditional environment may be just the thing for your gung ho camper. That introverted child who hates bugs of all kinds, group activities, and overnights at their best friend's house? Uh, maybe not.

While at first glance day or overnight camp seems a costly addition to your already financially challenged life, many camps offer "camperships." Ask. Look into programs run by the Y (day and overnight)—they're excellent and offer great value.

Most camps are anxious to get their bunks filled and will offer a discount if you sign up early in the season, or a cut rate for more than one child. (Note: Check the contract's cancellation and refund policy.) Conversely, as you get closer to summertime, if camps aren't full they may be willing to negotiate.

Salvation may be found through religious groups that often offer stipends if your child attends an affiliated camp; ask at your local church or synagogue or mosque.

Just as you're making time adjustments in other facets of your life—stretching time between hair coloring, for instance—consider shortening the time spent at camp: four instead of eight weeks, or two instead of four weeks. Beware of one-week overnight programs at all-around camps, however. Campers need time to adjust to being away from home and on their own, and one week is often not sufficient.

Finally, do the math: For working parents, overnight camp may present the best alternative to piecing together summertime child care.

Of course, if your child is older and has attended an overnight camp and she's dying to return, ask her to help defray the cost by babysitting or mowing yards in your neighborhood.

> **PUT THAT TAX CREDIT TO USE**
>
> **REMEMBER WE TALKED** about FSA dependent-care credits? Look into using this to help pay for summer day programs.

A SUMMER GROWTH SPURT

The best summer experiences give kids the chance to explore and grew. They gain independence by making choices and friendships out of sight of a parent's anxious and judging eye. Think about it: In this age of hovering helicopter parenting, sleepaway camp might be just the right antidote—providing you're not bunking in, too. Healthy separation is good for both you and your kiddo and leads to maturation and growth.

For some kids, summer camp is an opportunity to find and reinvent themselves. You know the meek nerdy boy at school, always the last one picked for basketball? Suddenly he blossoms as an expert water-skiing heartthrob. Or perhaps the same little kid goes to a more academic program and finds a place that feels like home. Summer friendships can last a lifetime. One of our dear friends met her husband at sports camp: During a rousing game of capture the flag, his fifteen-year-old heart was captured. It's stayed that way for decades.

CAMP CHECK

Wait, wait, wait.

Before you think we're shills for the summer camp industry, let us tell you we were camp semiquitters. At great financial sac-

rifice, our parents signed us up for Camp Chanrudemucka (or
something like that). The entire experience was miserable. The
rickety bunk, the leech-infested lake, no choice of activities, the
outhouse, and the mean counselor who was totally unsympa-
thetic to our menstrual distress. (Yes, we got our first period on
the second day of camp.)

Someone had not done her homework when she sent us to
this place—though it *was* truly a once-in-a-lifetime experience,
just like the brochure said. So be a good mama and do your
homework before you send your kids to any program. It doesn't
need to be perfect, but it needs to be good—and safe. Invest time
up front to make it a worthwhile investment for your little ones:

- If possible, visit the camp *in session.*
- Choose an American Camping Association–accredited
  program (www.acacamps.org/).
- Ask how long the current owners have run the program;
  new owners may be inexperienced and may have a large
  debt burden that diverts money from programming and
  staff.
- Ask for several references—and then call them all. Among
  the questions, ask what they like and don't like about the
  camp. How could it be better?
- Overnight programs should have a counselor-to-camper
  ratio of one to eight. Day programs should be one to ten.
  (This varies a little according to age group.) Most
  important, make sure you're comfortable with the ratios,
  and that your child has had experience with similar ratios
  in other settings.
- Ask about the average age of counselors. You want
  "seasoned" adults who have been there and done this
  before. Preferably teachers, coaches, youth leaders, etc.,

who do this for summer work. If the place is stewing with seventeen-years-olds in charge, be wary.

- Ask about (and double-check) the background screening they do for counselors.
- Is there a camp doctor on the grounds, or a registered nurse? How far is the nearest local hospital?
- Ask about the return rate of campers—you're looking for 65 to 70 percent. We're talking how many campers go back year after year. You want a camp with satisfied return customers.

For a busy mom on a budget, summer camps—day or overnight—are an opportunity for kids to learn in a convenient one-stop, no-carpool shop. Swimming, tennis, archery, painting, ceramics, music—there are so many kinds of summer activities and camps, you need to sort out which fit the bill for your child.

THE CAMP LADY

Most communities have someone known as the camp lady.

Your neighbor will tell you to call her; your cousin will have sent little Myrna to camp in the Adirondacks thirty years ago on her advice; the moms in line at Starbucks will tell you to see the camp lady if you're thinking about sending precious away.

By all means, go talk to your summer-camp lady. She'll have piles of pamphlets, soothing advice, and scads of sites for you to check into.

Just ask the camp lady how she makes her money. (We have no issue with everyone making a buck—hey, we're selling this book—but ask her how she is making her dough.) Does she get a bigger fee from certain camps? Are there camps that she doesn't represent because they don't pay her a fee? Does she lose her fee if your kid doesn't return? (If that is her answer, then that's not such a bad thing. It means she has an incentive to make a good match.)

FOR INFORMATION ON SLEEPAWAY OR DAY CAMPS

American Camp Association

YMCA camps

Audubon camps

Girl Scout camps

Boy Scout camps

SPECIALTY CAMPS

Let's say your teen is home for the entire summer, doing day jobs, taking local tennis lessons, etc., but has a passion for skateboarding. You might want to save to splurge (and she should be saving to splurge, as well) on a great summer specialty program. We're not in favor of this for little ones—they need broad exposure—but for your teen this may be the time to ignite and feed her passions.

Or say she's over the school choir. Enough renditions of Josh Groban's "You Raise Me Up"—this girl wants to *belt*. She's been practicing her guitar all school year—now she wants to make some noise with others like her. For more than ten years, Rock 'n' Roll Camp for Girls in Portland, Oregon, has been offering empowered, rockin' girls a weeklong experience they'll never forget. Okay, we know not everyone lives near Portland. No worries. There are now more than thirty-three members of the Girls Rock Camp Alliance offering great and affordable programs all across the country.

Mini-Francophile on your hands? Send him to French camp and he'll come home *très sophistique*—and with a crepe recipe that'll blow you away. Do you have a tennis, soccer, field hockey player anxious to hone her skills before the season begins? There's a camp for that.

GEEK POWER

BUDDING EINSTEIN OR Zuckerberg? See if your little genius qualifies for the Center for Talented Youth programs run by Johns Hopkins (http://cty.jhu.edu). One of ours found a home away from home in this academics-based summer camp program. The programs offer both need- and merit-based scholarships.

The immersion approach offered by specialty camps gives kids a rare and real taste of the field . . . be it sports, arts, technology, or academics. And the intensive, professional instruction rivals what they'll get at college, but (hopefully) in a less pressured environment. Since this is a good choice for older kids, they can help subsidize the bigger tuition or the cost of travel.

DIY CAMP

Just like you're exchanging clothing with friends and sharing babysitting duties for a free night out, consider banding together to organize summer activities for your same-aged kids. The success of the arrangement will depend on clear goals, rules, and organization.

Consider:

- How much child-care coverage do you need?
- What's the age range of the children?
- What activities interest each kid?
- What kind of access do you have to organized activities?

Sign the group up for community-offered tennis, swim, and soccer lessons. Take advantage of programs offered by local science and art museums. Use local playgrounds for games and picnics. Get a camera and have kids make a summer movie. Rainy days? Go to the movies in the morning. But remember that kids aren't made out of spun sugar and won't melt in the rain. A summer shower means popular parks empty out, so your gang gets the run of the place.

Think about having them volunteer at an assisted-living home or pet shelter. Make it fun. Keep them busy.

Take turns as camp leader, or think about hiring a known and trusted teacher as the groups' "counselor" for the summer. (Be neurotic. Don't send a bunch of kids off with anyone but a competent adult.)

FAMILY CAMP (NOT FAMILY CAMPING)

Ah, your favorite memories of summer camp—wouldn't it be great to reprise them? (No, we're not talking about making out with the CIT behind the arts-and-crafts cabin.) Inhale the piney processed-pancake breakfast smell in the mess hall. Hit the bull's-eye again on the archery field. Captain color wars. Water-ski.

Or you never went to camp but always wondered what it was like?

Consider family camp.

Never heard of it? The whole kit 'n' caboodle packs their duffels and heads out to the boonies for a weekend, a week. . . . How long would you go?

While we generally advocate low-cost, stay-at-home leisure activities like Rollerblading, playing cards, or cooking together, these are everyday and basic. Face it, every normal family has its share of dysfunction, and every family needs to shake it up, learn, and play together to continue growing and bonding.

Besides, where else can you find so many varied, healthy, fun activities sure to please everyone? Think of family camp as another opportunity to show kids it's never too late to learn something new or take a risk. Yes, even us elderly folks can rock-climb, learn to high-dive, scrape our knees, sing off-key by the campfire. . . .

We have friends who return year after year to the same camp to meet up with other returning families. Truth be told, we're kind of jealous. (Okay, not jealous enough to ever reprise our camp experience.)

Best of all for a mama on a budget, family camp offers a great value for a family vacation.

35

QUITTERS OFTEN PROSPER

So let's check in again. Where are we? Let's see, you're doing more playing with your kiddos at home. You're also letting them play by themselves. You're making sure they're physically fit and exposed to the arts. You're providing a balance between individual and group activities. You're nurturing their passions and latent skills, you're being a thoughtful role model, and you're showing them how to earn/save their own money for camp. You're teaching them about giving back, and letting them find their own comfort zone—

Now it's time to learn how to quit.

I QUIT

Everyone needs to learn to quit. Really, they do. Whether it's a bad job or a bad relationship, at some point in life you need the skills and the experience to say, "I'm out of here." Of course, the tricky issue is determining the right time for your child to throw in the towel, and how to help them learn from it. Think of extra-curricular games and lessons as an opportunity for them to hit the "quit" button—it's a low-cost way to learn a necessary life lesson. Hey, they can't quit the family and they can't quit school.

WHAT'S TOO MUCH?

Kids don't have the experience to know that new things are often frustrating, confusing, even disappointing. Hard work and per-severance often lead to great pleasure and payoff . . . but how can a five-year-old, seven-year-old, ten-year-old know that? It's your job to coach and encourage kids through the process of learning a new skill. (That's what you're doing when you're trying new things together.) It's also your job to help them know when it's okay to give it up, and to teach them to evaluate the pros and cons of such a decision.

Ideally, of course, we'd like to see a kid finish out a commit-ment: the sport season, the set of lessons, the camp session. But as adults, we also know that there are many things that aren't worth slogging through the sh*t for: a horrendous teacher, bul-lies in a group, inconsolable frustration. Sometimes a kid just isn't ready. Whether due to his or her makeup, family circum-stance, illness, stress—sometimes all the activities combined are just too much.

Start by helping them to sort out why they want to quit. Is it because they didn't get the part they wanted (Hamlet? quar-terback? prima ballerina)? Yes, that's disappointing, but that's life. Are they frustrated trying to learn a new skill (all thumbs on the piano, two left feet at soccer, tongue-tied onstage)? En-courage children to complete the season, group of lessons, or performance, and to look at it as a learning experience.

If their unhappiness is caused by more than not being the star of the show or not being a natural athlete or performer—say they're not getting playing time or are left out of the group or are being made fun of—then it's your job to help them. Start by facilitating a conversation with them and the coach or teacher.

In the end, you're the mom. If there's just too much psychic or physical pain involved (even if you think they're being overly sensitive—remember you're not them, and their feelings are real to them), by all means help find a graceful way out. Suggest that this isn't the year for soccer, violin, volleyball, but maybe they'd like to try it again another time. If your child is enrolled at a private facility and you've paid for lessons, negotiate a partial refund. If you believe that substandard adult supervision is the reason for their leaving, have a conversation with the director or owner of the facility and advocate for a full refund on that count. If you are participating through a town league or recreation program where coaches are volunteers, fold your tent and chalk it up to the cost of life.

In the end, offer your kids praise. Let them know how proud you are of them for understanding themselves well enough to know their limits and what they like and don't like. Encourage them to try something new.

OR NOT?

One of our kids spent a session at an overnight camp sending home the most original, artful, and piteous letters on why she needed to be rescued posthaste. Our favorite was the letter she thought would most tug at her foodie parents' hearts: The food was horrible, inedible, frightening! For God's sake, she wrote, they served iceberg lettuce! (Yes, the iceberg lettuce girl.) We flirted with the idea of rescuing her, but knew her to be an adaptive kid and so let her stay and bemoan the lettuce. She endured the three weeks. We brought her home and she skipped overnight camp for a few years. (She had not been ready—the iceberg lettuce was a red herring.) Then, at age thirteen, she wanted to give it another try. We investigated and found a camp that was opening that summer, which meant that all the campers would be new. A parent needs to be sensitive to the situation she's putting her child into, and a camp with returning campers in bonded bunks would not be ideal for a thirteen-year-old girl. She tried again. She had fun, learned new skills, and spent two summers as an outdoorsy gal. No letters home about lettuce (or arugula, for that matter). The point: She endured and persevered and quit and ended up trying again. (Who knew she'd package up all our points in one thrifty story?)

Years later, she did quit: nature, that is. She now lives in a big city, works in publishing (still a persuasive writer), and has no residual interest in the natural world.

YOU QUIT (OR SHOULD)

Sports, theater, music lessons, and art classes are add-ons in your already complicated life. They require paying, planning, driving, carpooling—not to mention time spent watching, cheering, encouraging, or nagging behind the scenes (did you practice the piano for thirty minutes today, Asa, really?). Often, while trying to do what is best for our kids, we take on more than we can handle. Like a boiling pot with a too-tight lid, the steam comes out the sides. Or we get a little overcooked and can't see clearly what is really going on. Sometimes you just need to say no. You are allowed to keep some unstructured, unscheduled time in your life!

WHAT A SMART MOM SHOULD KNOW

Parents can get a little confused about what their little ones are really learning in extracurriculars. We all have the nasty habit of getting stuck in the task itself and failing to see beyond the direct skill sets being taught. Your child is doing many other things besides learning how to hit the ball, strum the banjo, and dance the polka. They are experiencing different styles of teaching and other ways of learning, and meeting different groups of children beyond the local school or neighborhood. (They might even be having fun.)

One year one of our kids signed up to play a fall team sport, and every afternoon when we arrived to pick her up or watch the games she was sitting on the sideline. When we asked why, the reasons varied: She was tired; she didn't feel like it; she had a cramp in her side. In retrospect, we behaved badly (not the only time). We were too tired; we didn't feel like driving to get her; we had a cramp in our parenting brain. One day on the way home we read her the riot act: Don't play this sport again if you aren't going to play the sport!

What we missed was that no one (besides us) cared that she wasn't running up and down the field. Well, maybe the coaches looked at her slightly cross-eyed (which bothered us—not her), but she was doing serious socializing on the sidelines, and we didn't value it. In our task-driven frenzy we lost sight of the fact that she was *playing with her friends* and happy in ways that transcended kicking the ball or winning the game.

The lesson learned?

A smart mom never loses sight of what her kids really need: unconditional love, safe boundaries, and room to play. Then she gets the hell out of the way and gives them space to grow.

*I will see my children
for who they are.*

*I will separate my needs
from their needs.*

*I will ask them what
they would like to do.*

*I will not
overprogram them.*

*I will not
overprogram myself.*

*I will give them the opportunity
to try different activities.*

*I will encourage them
to persevere.*

*I will teach them
how to quit.*

*I will budget
everything but love.*

ABOUT THE AUTHOR

Rosalyn Hoffman is the author of *Bitches on a Budget: Sage Advice for Surviving Tough Times in Style*. She is a regular contributor to the Huffington Post, and she was a featured insider on the Daily Beast Buzz Board. A retail and marketing veteran, Roz was a buyer for Bonwit Teller, Filene's, and Lord & Taylor in New York City, and an executive for Avon and Lillian Vernon. She speaks Chinese and has traveled extensively in China. In addition to being a serious cook and wine collector, she has lived and studied cooking in France, and she has traveled the world cataloging changing markets. Aside from food and cooking, her other passion is design and architecture. She has worked with award-winning architects in the building and design of several modern homes that have garnered awards and international recognition. Roz is the mom of two recent college graduates, who are gainfully employed, self-supporting and happily surviving all on their own.